Praise For *Be*

Master Life Coach Chris Scott is an Anointed Writer, she has been a source of inspiration and hope for thousands of people all over the world. I can trust that whenever she releases another book it's going to be impactful as her voice carries unadulterated truth on every subject.

This book *Beyond the Smile* is a sensational account of 13 women and their journey and experience during the COVID-19 pandemic and other issues that they have endured.

I am confident their testimonies will be transformative and inspirational.

> *Proverbs 15:30*
> *A cheerful look brings joy to the heart; good news makes for good health.*

Tongela Smith
IMPACT Life Coaching and Mediation Service
www.IamTongelaSmith.org

"Become the Most Successful You"

BEYOND THE SMILE

Chris Scott Ministries

Chris Scott, Chris Scott Ministries

ISBN: 978-1-7360211-0-1 (Paperback)
ISBN 978-1-7360211-1-8 (eBook)

Edited by Christine Bode
Book Cover Design by Trevor Bailey
Book Production by Dawn James, Publish and Promote
Design and Layout by Perseus Design

Photo Courtesy List
Ynwanda Market: Nara Meas Photography
LaQuanda Plantt: Lyndon Winchester
Kenyatta Collins: K. Renee Photography LLC
Ashley Brittney: Kristen Hall Photography
Sharon Jones: Front Page Photography
Zen Watson: Deshaun Watson Phillips

Printed and bound in the United States of America

Note to the reader: The events in this book are based on the writers' memories from their perspective. Certain names have been changed to protect the identity of those mentioned. The information is provided for educational purposes only. In the event you use any of the information in this book for yourself, which is your constitutional right, the author and publisher assume no responsibility for your actions.

Contents

Foreword

There is no greater healing than feeling seen, heard, supported, and forgiven. Just when I thought it was almost impossible to find all those qualities in one vessel, I had the pleasure of meeting the anointed, Minister Chris Scott! When a mutual friend introduced me to Chris, (regarding a space to train kids interested in entertainment), I knew immediately she would be a forever friend, now turned sister. Her benevolence was (and still is) second to none. She literally, would not let me give her a dime in compensation for the space. I remember thinking, "Who is this woman? What's the catch? How can she be so generous?" Then I realized, this is what an angel on earth looks like; a woman who truly walks the walk.

This book is another testament for the heart and soul of someone who continues to SEE, HEAR, SUPPORT, AND FORGIVE so many. Rather than taking center stage and writing about other women who are survivors, leaders, and examples of overwhelming triumph, Ms. Scott's divine intuition knew that allowing women to write their own stories would help heal those who write and the many who would read their real-life "SHERO STORIES."

One of my favorite quotes is "Great people make other people great." Thank you, my sister, my production partner, and my personal life coach for helping me and so many others to find and stay on a path of greatness. I love you with my whole heart.

Charmin Noel Lee
Actor, producer, director, creator of "Book It" master class

Introduction

This book is the result of 12 amazing women who accepted the challenge and made a decision to allow the world to take a peek "Beyond the Smile" they wear so well. They each hold a special place in my heart. As I think of them, I think of beautiful flowers in God's garden.

Several months ago, the Holy Spirit gave me the title of this book. I took time and wrote down ten titles which included *Beyond the Smile*, but wanted to allow the co-authors to help select the right one. Although I knew what God had already spoken, I sent them all ten titles and asked that they each select the three top choices. God had spoken again as the top choice was *Beyond the Smile*, after the second round of voting.

Let's go a little deeper on the choice in naming the book. The women in this compilation of amazing stories tell their truths of smiling while hurting and wounded. I sometimes call it, "serving while hemorrhaging." Many women can relate to living their daily lives while much is going on within, but yet they smile. There are many times that we endure betrayal, negativity, and fear, yet we still smile. Most of the time, those closest to us don't even know what is going on within the depths of our souls.

These women of strong FAITH, who I affectionately call Queens, have emptied themselves onto paper and have discovered the therapeutic necessity of telling their truth to bless other women. The launching of this book was as though we each released a thousand doves. It is a symbolization of freedom and self-awakening. God created for us, a sister circle of support for one another that will live forever. We each found strength and confidence in prayer and the love that has been displayed, birthed victory in abundance. Sit back, grab your warm throw blanket and a glass of your favorite drink as we go "Beyond the Smile" of my co-authors Ashley Brittney, Consuelo Allen, Detral Williams, Kenyatta Collins, LaQuanda Plantt, Mia Colemon, Michelle Hudson, Renata Triblett, Sharon P. Jones, Zen Watson, Tonya Clinton, and Ynwanda S. Market.

Proverbs 31:14-20 (NIV)

She is like the merchant ships,
bringing her food from afar.
She gets up while it is still night;
she provides food for her family
and portions for her female servants.
She considers a field and buys it;
out of her earnings she plants a vineyard.
She sets about her work vigorously;
her arms are strong for her tasks.
She sees that her trading is profitable,
and her lamp does not go out at night.
In her hand she holds the distaff
and grasps the spindle with her fingers.
She opens her arms to the poor
and extends her hands to the needy.

CHAPTER 1

Caught in the Crossfire

by Chris Scott

The car in front of me came to a screeching halt, the driver mashing on his breaks to escape the gunfire. Little did I realize that I was right in the line of fire. I honked my horn desperately for the driver in front of me to keep moving, but he froze not knowing what to do. I was trapped and terrified. The first bullet hit my driver's side car door. I was stuck. I watched helplessly as the young man in the blue t-shirt ran in my direction as the gunman fired his .38 caliber revolver hoping that one of his bullets would hit the runner in his back and take him out. It was 6:30 a.m. and the sun was just coming up on 107th Street and 32nd Avenue. I had woken up early and packed my four-door sedan full of goods to sell at the Sunrise Flea Market as I did every Saturday for years. I decided to take the local roads. I drove from Northern Blvd; not aware I was entering a war zone from a drug deal gone bad. As I approached the top of the hill everything started to move in slow motion. My life started to flash before my eyes. As the second bullet hit the bottom driver's side of my car door, I saw myself sitting on the front step of my parents' store. My life was flashing before me.

Flashback

There was always much going on "Beyond the Smile" that everyone adored, even as a little girl growing up. That day while smiling at the patrons as they entered and exited the store as I often did, a strange woman I had not remembered seeing before, came and sat next to me. My parents were busy tending to their regular customers and conducting business in the shop. The lady spoke words to me that I don't remember to this day. She seemed warm and genuine and I could have been easily whisked away with her charm. It was not until much later in my life that I realized the danger that I may have been in. I really can't recall what made her leave, but it could have been an approaching customer. I was told that I was a pretty little girl with an engaging smile that everyone loved. My parents normally paid close attention to my whereabouts, but when the store became busy that was much more difficult to do. Later that evening I became very ill and my parents had me transported to the local hospital. The halls of Port of Spain General seemed cold and the metal bed rails and the thin mattress did not seem welcoming. That night, and for the next few days, the doctors worked diligently to discover what was going on with me. They said they had never seen such symptoms before. My parents began to worry, especially when the doctors said they couldn't do anything else for me and they felt my parents should prepare for the worse. I remember my mother crying and I could not understand what was happening, as my little body was ravished with pain and I was drenched in sweat. I remember having a bad, persistent cough.

My father told me later in life that my mother cried herself to sleep that night, but while she slept God gave her a vision that provided the answers to my illness. She dreamt about what was attacking my frail little body. When my parents returned to the hospital the next morning and shared what was told to my mother the night before, the doctors were astonished. God spoke to my mother and made it clear to them and they were then able to treat me for my ailment, which was known as whooping cough. Whooping cough, also known as pertussis, is a highly contagious disease that affects the lungs. Anyone exposed to the bacteria can get sick. Sometimes I wonder if I had contracted it from the strange woman on the step.

One year after that incident, my father immigrated to the United States. I remembered when they told us he was leaving and that my mother would join him in six months. Six months seemed like a distance away, but it came quicker than I could imagine. The time came and both my parents were miles away, on what seemed like another planet. It would be almost a year before I could join them. The time I spent without my parents was very difficult. I encountered things that I choose not to give many details about in this book. I may never come to terms with it, but I have learned to forgive those that hurt me as a little girl and teenager. I will say this, what an older cousin forced me to do was not what childhood is about. Well, he has gone on to eternity now and I never told my parents, due to the fear of confusion, although I was too young to understand why he ejaculated in the sink right in front of me after forcing my five-year-old hand to caress his penis.

Life in Queens

I was five years old when I landed at John F. Kennedy International Airport in Queens, New York. I traveled with my oldest brother, who was 16 years old at the time. He took good care of me. We had a stop in Barbados where we met another cousin. It was my first time traveling abroad. I did not fully understand the new life we were stepping into but was excited to get on the plane. The airline flight attendants were kind and all of them looked like models back then. They complimented me on my smile. As the plane took off down the runway, I became filled with excitement, knowing that I would soon be in the arms of my mother and father. I also felt a sense of relief that I was leaving an uncomfortable situation behind. At five years old, I didn't understand what it meant to be violated but was happy to get as far away as possible from the violator. Crossing the ocean would not be far away enough.

We left Barbados after a four-hour layover and were once again on our way to America. The airport was very busy, unlike anything I had been used to. There were all types of people moving busily about. Little did I know that one day I would work at that same airport as a young adult. My brother handled getting us through customs, which I later realized was not easy for him at 16 years old as it was his first time traveling abroad as well. The immigration area was completely sealed off by frosted glass doors and tall windows. Dogs were sniffing about and men and women were dressed in uniforms. The customs officer searched through our hand luggage to discover the bottles of Caribbean goodies and homemade pepper sauce sent by my grandmothers. They questioned my brother and I guess he gave them the right answers because we were told to keep moving. We stood before the tall white doors, anticipating they would open and that my parents would be standing there, awaiting our arrival. The electric doors opened, and a cold breeze fiercely hit my body. I expected my parents to be right there but to my amazement, there were people much further away behind a roped-off area. There were so many people, I could not sift through the crowd to find my parents. I became instantly overwhelmed by the crowd and strange faces. I thought it was a different planet. My brother grabbed my hand and moved me along, being careful so that I would not get trampled. Then I heard a voice call my name; a voice familiar to my heart. Then a male voice called my brother's name. My eyes searched the crowd as I tried to follow the path of the familiar sound of a man and a woman. Finally, I saw my parents and ran to them. My mother began to cry as she hugged me and did not want to let go. We continued to walk through the airport and my mother put a heavy coat on me. She wrapped a scarf around my mouth and put on knitted mittens. My father went ahead to get the car. I watched as the long, light blue station wagon pulled alongside the curb. We climbed in and headed towards my new life in America.

I was jolted back to reality as the last bullet just missed my window and the car in front of me began to move beyond the intersection. I immediately began to thank God for protecting me and shielding me from danger. Could you imagine being caught and trapped in the crossfire? I could not move or get out of the car. God loves me that much and at that moment after returning to reality, I concluded that he had much more for me to accomplish for his kingdom.

Journey to Florida

It was January of 1997 when my husband and I decided we would sell our house and move to Florida. Our income had been reduced to minimal. He had a good career for the railroad bringing in six figures and I was successful in my career. It was a cold winter morning when he broke the news to me that he had been laid off. We were devastated but didn't know that God had other plans. It was a set-up for our good even though the set-up caused us to endure some very tough times. About six months later, we packed up our little red car with as much as we could fit in it. The moving men had come, and we packed up the truck with what seemed like all that we owned. We were expected to arrive in two weeks to begin our new life. The house in New York was a very small, three-bedroom house with a nice cozy basement, worth about $250,000 (we discovered later on that this tiny house sold for just under one million dollars, nine years after we sold it). We lived five minutes from LaGuardia Airport and 20 minutes outside of Manhattan. It was a difficult decision to leave the city where we both grew up but knew that we needed a change. My mother came over to say her "see you laters" and cried, but felt a sense of comfort since we were moving to the area where she had built a house and would one day live near us again. With our two daughters, we headed to Florida, drove through New Jersey, Delaware, and arrived in Lorton, Virginia that afternoon. We pulled up to the huge train and the car was driven onto the ramp. It took us 16 hours to arrive in Sanford, Florida (not knowing that one day the name Trayvon Martin would make the city famous with the loss of his innocent life). The drive from Sanford to Port St. Lucie was one of excitement but was also filled with fear of the unknown. I had not lived outside of New York City, other than my first five years in Trinidad and Tobago.

AC and I had decided that I would go back to New York after one week and continue working as a real estate agent. I was very successful at what I did at the firm. I was awarded the #1 listing agent for several terms. The plan was that I would stay just a short time and send money home until AC got a job. However, my first lesson was that our plans are not God's plans. I headed back to New York and was soon back at work selling property at ERA Home King. I will tell anyone to this day that you should never separate from your spouse for a long time. It was not the best decision we made. While the money was coming in and we were financially "making it", my husband and children still needed me to be physically there.

There were a pastor and his family that lived close by and they had invited my family to church one day. They ended up becoming members of this very small family-oriented ministry. The pastor and his wife became like family. They helped as much as they could during my absence. I would travel to Florida for a weekend, once a month. I became comfortable with living in New York and started changing my mind about relocating. I had an excuse every month about why I should stay in New York. My family was hurting because I wasn't there with them, but I soon realized that the enemy had me right where he wanted me. Confused and blind, "Beyond the Smile!" While my husband and children's Sundays consisted of a powerful message by the pastor, mine consisted of showing houses and gaining clients. I was stagnant in the Word and my relationship with God was one-sided. The enemy was having a field day and I could not see beyond the money. I began to isolate myself from the family that still lived in New York, from my in-laws and anyone that I had been connected to outside of work. I even stopped associating with my friends in my theater career as an actress. Yet God was talking to me, but I could not hear him. It was not until I had a dream that things began to change, and the spiritual scales began to fall off my eyes. I laid in my bed in that tiny apartment in Brooklyn and stared at the moon outside my window as the tears began to flow. As I looked at the moon, a longing to be with my husband and my children came over me. I tell you, when the enemy is out to get you, he will first try to spiritually blind you! I kept thinking and wondering if my girls still loved me and if they were staring at the same moon.

It had been almost a year and AC was working at a local hospital. The girls were now in middle and high school. One night my husband had gone with church members to visit another church in an area called Pahokee, just on the other side of the Okeechobee River. It was pouring rain and in the car with him, were our two girls and other children from the youth ministry. The rain became blinding and he could barely see the road in front of him. If you have never experienced Florida rain, you may not want to. Immediately, the car went off the side of the dark, lightless road, and the children began to scream. AC shouted "Jesus", beyond all the chaos. The pandemonium in the car was heart-wrenching, but at the name of Jesus, the car was lifted back onto the road and my husband was able to regain control. I remember AC telling me that it was as though angels lifted the car and placed it back on the road. He was sure it was a mighty move of God! They made it safely to the destination. After he told me about the experience, that night I dreamt of a prayer circle lead by my mother-in-law who lives in the Bronx. She has a circle of prayer warriors that have been friends for over fifty years. In the dream, they had made a circle around AC and me and prayed for us with urgency. That next morning God spoke clearly to me when he warned that if I did not leave to join my family in Florida immediately, I would lose them. I called AC that morning, sobbing, and told him I was coming home. I wish I had time to go into the journey to the Sunshine State because a lot was going on, "Beyond the Smile!"

My Calling

It was in the Sunshine State where I realized that God was calling me to help others. It was not the ordinary kind of help; he had called me for something special. First, I had to overcome the series of challenges I encountered with the separation by distance in my marriage. Through God using my husband to teach me how to forgive myself for past mistakes, the discovery of my "calling" started to manifest itself.

Our Father, God, has a sense of humor, but it's all for our good. Growing up, it seemed like I was always trying to be the perfect friend to others, especially to women. I remember when I was 17 years old and my friend and I accepted part-time employment with a company selling newspaper subscriptions via the telephone. We had to use the Yellow Pages (if you can remember those phone books back then) to search for a series of numbers and call those people. We worked evening hours when people were said to be home from work. Well, my friend had a heavy accent because she had just moved from Dominica, West Indies. We were quite close and our parents were friends as well. I remember her being fired from that summer job because she was not making enough sales, due to her accent being a major hindrance. Well, guess what I did? Yes, I spoke to the boss and said, "If she goes, then I go." She kept her job, right? Wrong! He said goodbye and watched as we both left the office. While I lost the job, I felt good about my decision because I stood up for my friend. For the next few months, we both sat at home, jobless. She became employed before me. If I had to make that decision today, things may go a little differently. I am happy to say that she is a successful attorney that makes enough money to purchase that little dump today if she wanted to.

After being hurt in friendships with women, I vowed that I didn't want to deal with them beyond my best friend Simone. We have been friends for over 30 years. She was a spunky, radical college student returning to New York from Clark Atlanta University. We met while auditioning for a role at the Black Spectrum Theater. We are still friends today. You know the type of friend that you can pick up the phone and have a conversation with as though it were yesterday? Yeah, that kind of friend.

Well God had other plans, "Beyond the Smile!" I remember I used to get easily offended when people would say and do things that were not nice. I am being too kind here. They did things that were rude and mean! These were Christians behaving like this (I still encounter them today, but have learned to speak directly to those demons in them). Well one day, I asked God, "Father, God, please deliver me from people." He led me to what is now my favorite scripture: Psalms 119:165 (KJV) ***Great peace have they which love thy law: and nothing shall offend them.*** I recited this scripture over and over until it connected with my entire being. I must warn you to be careful about asking God to deliver you from that thing you are struggling with because he will test you over and over again until you have been delivered. That year I went through the wringer with women and deception. So much that I decided to direct a stage play for my friend called *Deception*. How appropriate. God started to develop in me a strong will and the ability to see beyond the actions of people. I learned a new level of forgiveness. He started sending women my way for mentorship and to love them as a mother and big sister.

It was when we relocated to Georgia that the women's ministry in me became evident. My desire to help and mentor beautiful souls for the kingdom of God grew. Don't get me wrong, hurt still occurs, but I would not give up on what God has called me to be in the lives of others. I think God has graced me with a special kind of love for others. The kind that looks within and sees the beautiful flower ready to bloom on the inside. I somehow see "Beyond the Smile."

ABOUT THE AUTHOR

Professor Chris Scott is an entrepreneur, Master Life Coach, global community leader, author and minister. She is the founder of SoReal Productions, a performing arts and film company dedicated to telling rich and powerful stories that make a positive impact. She is also the founder of SoReal Life Solutions, which focuses on helping people pursue and enhance their life goals through coaching, counseling and education. As a master life coach, Professor Scott trains life coaches from around the world. Through her life coaching training program, Global Connections Academy and other Life Coaching Schools, she has trained and certified over 500 life coaches.

From 2014-2019, Professor Scott served as President and CEO of the Caribbean Association of Georgia, Inc., (CAG). During her tenure, Chris led the organization into relationships that supported the organizational mission of helping others, building cultural awareness while growing the reach of CAG. Chris also focused on increasing support for children, seniors, veterans, the homeless, students and locally underserved communities.

Professor Scott is the author of the book, *Discovering Your Spiritual Gifts! Connecting the Dots to Your Purpose* and the journal, *Good Morning My Sister.* She is the creative force behind the anthology, *Treasures in My Heart* recognized as an Amazon Best Seller and #1 New Release. Her books are now available in stores and libraries in South Africa, Trinidad and Tobago, The Bahamas and throughout the United States. Her fourth, "Beyond the Smile" will be released in the next few months.

Professor Scott is also the owner and creative director of Trinity Performing Arts Academy. She has also served as director, producer and executive producer on several films and stage productions. Professor Scott has also received numerous honors for service and the arts. In 2015, she was presented with the President's Volunteer Service Award under the Barack Obama Administration. In 2017, she won the Director and Producer of the Year awards from Diamondnique Productions. In 2018, she was awarded the community service award for Woman on Fire for her work as a missionary. Professor Scott was honored by the Atlanta Dream, WNBA team and presented an award by the owner Kelly Loeffler for most Aspiring Woman.

She is a licensed and ordained minister who serves at Tabernacle of Praise Church International where she leads their global mission's team and has led missionary trips to Haiti, Belize, Jamaica, South Africa, Trinidad and Tobago and Dominican Republic. She also is a member of the leadership team of Living Sacrifice Prophetic Ministry in Trinidad and Tobago. Chris has more than 20-years of experience mentoring ministry consultants, apostles, bishops and pastors.

Professor Scott's passion for people extends beyond the borders. It also includes marriage and family. Chris & her husband, Chaplain AC, lead a marriage ministry called, "Loving You Until." Their work together allows them to counsel couples both married and dating. They have also created Global Connections Academy and Global Connections Ministries International to train life coaches and to meet the needs of churches seeking to build their global missions. They are the CEOs of Coaching Forward International (CFI).

Chris has been married 33 years and shares three wonderful children and four amazing grandchildren with husband, AC Scott. To learn more about Chris Scott and her work visit www.chrisscott.net.

CHAPTER 2

Rejected at Birth

by Tonya Clinton

Births are supposed to be exciting. Celebrating the entrance of a new life, a new legacy, and all the new possibilities. New arrivals usually usher in family gatherings and curiosities of what the baby looks like. Imagine aunties crowded around a baby, making a big fuss about who will hold the baby. In my family, it is always my Auntie Pat that decides to take the role of checking the ears. You see, the ears are very important because the top of the ears was said to determine the color of the baby. Aunt Linda liked to take the role of the beauty predictor, meaning, she could gauge the beauty of a baby like a thermometer: low, moderate, or hot, to determine if the baby was going to be beautiful or just ugly. Those are the precious memories that I have of my family gathering after the birth of a baby.

All of that would have been super exciting, but in my case, my mother drove herself to the hospital, alone. She lay in the hospital room, alone. And she gave birth to me alone with no one in the room. My mother's name was the only name on my birth certificate. There would be no family gathering and loud conversations about the color of my baby ears or even the prediction of how I would look in the years to come. There was only room enough for loud silence. This type of silence is weighty, and it sinks in so deeply and stretches itself so wide to intrude and insist that it stays.

It was December 1973, and just like it was almost winter time, my mother was almost married. The word almost is very tricky, kind of like blowing up a balloon, taking one breath after another until it looks like a balloon, and then when you try to secure it, somehow the balloon gets away, becoming unreachable, spiraling out of control until there is nothing left...wasted air. Tricky is somewhat like when I was little, and my older brother Troy would ask me if I wanted some of his ice cream, seemingly sincere, as he told me how good his ice cream was, yummy even. Then, as I began to lean forward in anticipation of the chilled treat, he moved his cone out of the way leaving my mouth gaped open, tasting only the air. My father and mother were engaged, but he decided to move on with his life without having the decency to notify my mother. Adding salt to the wound, everyone in town knew about my father getting married. In fact, her best friend didn't even tell her. When my grandfather found out and brought the news to my mother, it was the day of her supposed fiancé's wedding to another woman. It was a hot day in South Georgia when my grandfather told my mother this news, and I would think that this type of news would be given when a person was sitting down; however, he just told her. She didn't faint, and she didn't cry, but she did make a personal pledge that she would not depend on him to raise their two children. She did just that. Just like the tide being gravitated by the moon, she was pulled up north to New York City with two kids in tow, but unlike rocks skipped across the water, creating ripples that expand exponentially, the effect of these ripples lasted for generations.

How could someone make raising two kids alone look so effortless? Having left a place of weighty silence in South Georgia to live on busy 131st Street in a Lionel Hampton in Harlem, NYC proved that it is the city that never sleeps, as my mother barely shut her eyes. She worked by day and attended college at night. I knew her as a momma, but I had no clue about how much she sacrificed for my brother and me. Unfortunately, she did it alone, because my father probably paid more for eating out monthly than he sent her for child support. If fatherhood was like school and attendance was taken, my father would have been considered absent. There would be no break for my mother, not a summer away, not two weeks away, not even a day of reprieve to relieve the stress of working so hard. My mom was all work and no play. Now, I recognize the voice that drove her to work so hard. It was the voice of rejection.

In Dispose

I remember asking my mom questions about my father. Interestingly enough I never really thought about what I lacked because I was always filled with the love provided by my mother and brother. We were like an entire posse, in and of ourselves. Questions about my father began one February afternoon after I received an envelope in the mail. I saw my name written neatly in black ink. There was an artistic vibe to this handwriting; very unique. I remember thinking, "I have a father? Who is he?" I only knew his name, but just the mere thought of receiving an envelope in the mail from my father caused me to grin from ear to ear. I did a quick dance with the envelope in my hand. My body moved one way, and my ponytails another. This new awakening broke the silence. I became inquisitive and asked my mother questions. She never really volunteered information about my father, but she never held back any information either. When my brother and I would ask questions, she would answer the question with the right amount of information. Not too little and not too much. Getting something out of my mother was like prying open a box with folded indentations that indicated they wanted to be closed shut. She never said anything negative about my absent father. There were many things that a single mom could say, but she always kept the peace, leaving it to my brother and me to figure it out for ourselves.

On the day that I asked for my father's number, my mother wrote it down on a blank sheet of paper. I remember thinking that my relationship with my father was just like this sheet of paper… blank…as blank as the space where his name should have been on my birth certificate. I had no point of reference, and at the age of seven, I wanted to hear his voice. What did he sound like? Questions raced through my head like crazy drivers determined to make it to their destination. On this day, I was determined to call him. I remember sitting on my mother's canopy bed where I closed my eyes and took a deep breath. I quickly picked up the phone with my sweaty little palms and began to dial slowly. 9…1…2…and carefully dialed the rest of the numbers. I waited patiently for someone to pick up the phone, and while it seemed like an eternity, on the third ring, someone picked up. I quickly smiled when I heard a woman's voice on the other end. I heard "Hello" in a deep southern accent. My voice was shaky because I was so nervous, but I was finally able to utter these words, "Can I speak to my father?" I wasn't sure what to ask. Should I ask for him by his first and last name? Do I call him Mister? Do I ask for Dad? I had to think quickly. After a long pause, I said, "Hello?" in a questioning way. I wondered if the lady who answered the phone was still on the line. The voice asked, "Who is this?" I quickly piped up and said, "This is Tonya," with excitement that was met by a scowling voice, full of disdain. I heard the lady on the other end say, "He's in DISPOSE!!!" It sounded like she said it with a frown. At seven years old, what did I know about disposal? On the toilet? Busy? Out? Not available? Disappointed, I replied, "OK, thank you," and quickly got off the phone. Unfortunately, this dispose thing would continue from year to year. I didn't know that my father could be in dispose that much. I felt rejected, yet again, with no access to a father. The voice of rejection would speak to me saying, "You see, you don't have a father. He doesn't want you… you see, he is always busy."

The Wrong Touch

A couple of years passed but I continued to dream of being called Daughter, of being called beautiful, and of being validated. I decided that I wanted more than what my mother and brother had to offer. I wanted what almost every kid at my school in the East Bronx had, a father.

At the age of 11, I was taller than everyone in my class, with chocolate smooth skin, and a contagious smile. My two front teeth refused to conform to the rest of my mouth and protruded a little. My legs never seemed to stop growing; legs everlasting. I was more tomboy than a lady, and raced, ran hard, and played until the streetlights came on. My main friends consisted of some kids on our block. I had Puerto Rican friends, Irish friends, Italian friends, and Yugoslavian friends. I loved the freedom of going outside and playing. Our closest friend Rodney lived downstairs. His parents were Jamaican immigrants and they were our landlords, who I viewed as an extra set of grandparents. They seemed like family to me. During Christmas, Mrs. P would make rum cakes placed in tin cans like the kind that cookies come in. She even made us snacks from time to time when my mother was working late. They kept an eye on us and it wasn't anything for us to go downstairs to visit them.

I never forgot the day I went downstairs looking for my friend because I wanted to play. Mrs. P told me to go downstairs to the basement because my friend was down there. When I went downstairs, Mr. P was sitting on the couch working on something. I asked him where my friend was and Mr. P asked me to, "come here for a second." He asked me to come a little closer because he wanted to show me something. I didn't think anything of it, so I proceeded to move closer. He then asked me to sit down next to him and I did. I honestly didn't have a point of reference, as he was like a grandfather to me. He then reached over and touched me in my private area, and tried to stick his old tongue in my mouth. The place he touched belonged to me and my lips belonged to me as well. I was throwing up on the inside. As I sat there, a thousand thoughts raced through my young mind. Why? What was going on? What did I do to deserve this? It is my fault because I should have known not to come closer. I sat there in utter shock and disgust. Although those nasty touches lasted about two minutes, I remember the two questions that he asked me. With his strong Jamaican accent, he asked, "Do you like this? Does it feel good?" Suddenly, at the sound of footsteps and movement on the top of the steps, the violation ended as quickly as it began. Before I could fully run out of the door, I remember him calling my name. He put his finger up to his old wrinkled lips, motioned, "Shh..." and said that the secret was between us. Fear gripped my heart. What had just happened and why? Did I make him do that? He was my only father figure and I quite honestly trusted him. Needless to say, I never went back downstairs again.

Summer passed and with the approach of fall, my mother sat us down and told us that we would be moving soon because we had been evicted. Our landlords had increased our rent twice in a couple of months. Then Mr. P told my mom that the apartment was needed for a family member. I could not help but think that it was my fault that we had to move. I kept hearing the echo of the SHHH...and visualizing his wrinkled finger in front of his lips. This was the beginning of my silence. I was bound, not because of my doing, but because of what someone else decided to do to me. I had a victim's eyes... Do you know that the eyes of a victim can speak loudly even if their mouths are taped shut? It would be years before I whispered what had happened, to my mother. To add insult to the injury of rejection, I had just been violated and victimization and shame ushered into my life. At this point, Rejection introduced me to his partners in crime, and they are called Victimization and Shame.

My mother took yet another deep breath and moved my brother and me from the Bronx to Far Rockaway in Queens. Still in search of my identity, middle school I.S. 53, surely did not help me find it. Whew, from Day 1, I was teased. This was the school of hard knocks and my transition from a predominately white school to the inner city left me muted. At this school, I was called names that my mother didn't give me, such as Squeaky because of my high-pitched voice, and Teen Wolf because my hair was so thick. I didn't roll with the crowd. I was quiet, but I still wanted to belong. I didn't want to hang out with the girls who fought all the time, because my mother would kill me. I didn't want to hang out with the girls who were already engaging in sex in the eighth grade, because again, my mother would kill me. So, my next best option was to hang with the skippers, and I skipped school. I should have known that God had his hand on my life because I always got caught. The Holy Spirit would reveal that I was either in trouble or about to be in trouble. My mom gave me two, week-long punishments, and when I violated my two-week punishment by going outside when she was at work, the punishments increased to an entire month. After many punishments, I started to read books, drink hot tea, and watch Oprah in the afternoon. Looking back, I am grateful for the punishment, but at this point in my life, I felt isolated.

High school was full of sacrifices and transitions. We moved again, back to the South, to slow down the pace. My life changed after getting saved in the ninth grade, and I gave my first sermon at the age of 16. My time was spent in prayer and worship, and it was all things church, but rejection would rear its ugly head again because I still wanted to belong and to be validated by my natural father.

Overlooked

I remember a time when I was a teenager in high school, and I had the opportunity to hang out with my older half-brothers for the day. They had driven down from Atlanta, Georgia to Tallahassee, Florida, and they came to pick me up. I belonged. I remember laughing and joking with them all day into the early afternoon. My older brothers had a way of making me feel seen, visible, connected to my father's side of the family. Again, I never wanted to cause any trouble or stir any waters, I simply wanted to belong. I made up my mind that I would listen more than talk. I would smile and be agreeable with a simple nod, or a yes, whatever you say. Whatever you want to eat, I am not picky. Whatever you want to give me because I appreciate you so much for allowing me into your world. I remember nodding and grinning throughout my trip from Tallahassee, Florida to Moultrie, Georgia, for one and a half hours. We were not just sightseeing; this visit had a purpose. We were going to see my father. I was simply amazed that the day had come for me to drive my father's town to see him. I was 17 years old, a senior in high school, taking dual enrollment classes at a community college. But I was missing something quite fundamental. I had never been to my father's house and could not help but think about what it looked like. Was I more like him, or my mom? The very moment that I had proof of his existence was when I had received the Valentine's Day card he had sent. My imagination took me back to the age of seven and the smell of the card. Why in the world did I smell the card? Maybe I thought I could trace him. My focus returned to the present and the highways that led me to South Georgia; lone highways surrounded by green fields, green treetops, and blank landscape. I couldn't help but think that these roads would lead me to a place I always longed for – "Belonging," where I was called a daughter.

Although my brothers never told me that we were going to my father's house, I assumed that we would go there. Remember, I was just a smiling passenger and I felt good to belong, at least for that moment. We drove through the city limits of small-town Georgia, and my brothers slowed down and made a quick right turn into the parking lot of a community college. It was the place of my father's job, after his retirement. I could not help but feel the butterflies in my stomach. My dad, the educator. Maybe this would connect the dots to my love of books; why I look or act the way I do. Validation…just a simple nod would do.

As my brothers and I entered the building, coolness hit my face along with a determination to see my dream come true. What would come out of this? Would it be daddy-daughter brunches? Maybe I would be invited over for Sunday dinner, Thanksgiving, or Christmas with my brothers? Instead of imagining the time that I would have with my dad, I was there, standing next to my brothers. It was mystical and I was exuberant. I was the Kool-Aid kid, all smiles and nodding away. Anything that was said, I was agreeable to, because again, I wanted to belong. These short moments seemed like an eternity to the 17-year-old girl who had longed and waited. Within that short period, a conversation took place between my father and brothers; simple small talk. I felt awkward because I was looking for a little more of, "Hey Girl, look at You!" But instead, I received a very mellow, "Hello." I was still bewildered by the fact that I was there. I continued to pay close attention to my small breaths, so I wouldn't faint from amazement. One of my father's coworkers entered the room and I will never forget his question. "Who do we have here?" My father's voice developed some excitement as he quickly and enthusiastically introduced brother one and brother two, and sister-in-law. And then he took a deep breath, but instead of him saying the words I had always longed to hear, he held his breath in silence. In retrospect, I do not question why he didn't acknowledge me. He will have to answer to God for that, but I do question why I continued to nod and smile, with my head held high. My thoughts collided: "Can I go now? Did anyone catch that he omitted something or someone impertinent – me? Who am I now?" I remembered my mom saying, "I will never say anything bad about your father, you will determine things for yourself." The time had come, and the resemblance of chocolate skin and high cheekbones, with a bottom flat lip, was not enough to call me Daughter. I would never forget the pause in the room…the quiet, questioning space in the white coworker's eyes, eyebrows formed a question mark. Unfortunately, what was supposed to have been the greatest day of my life, was a painful day that fragmented my soul.

Compromise and College Years

I remember feeling lonely, although I was young, saved, and I loved God. I knew a whole lot about spirituality but did not know how to have fun. Everybody was having fun… living their best lives. I wanted not only to belong but to learn how to enjoy my life and embrace friendships. All I understood was hard work, survival, and being a devil slayer, which is great, but balance is key. I remember looking at all the college students laughing, having fun, and hanging out. I will never forget when I was asked in high school by one of the coolest football players if I wanted to be a nun when I grew up. I remembered being shocked by that question… like… um. I squinched my nose, and pushed my lips out, exclaiming aloud, "No!" I quickly told him that yes, I was close to God. No, I would not live a life of solitude.

I remember losing my focus and instead of meditating on Godly things, I began to dream of having a boyfriend. After all, everybody else had one. It would be years later, after failed friend-ships, a failed marriage, and two kids, when I realized that my life paralleled my mother's life. I had made the same pledge that I could and would raise my children to the best of my ability and I would not fail no matter what. I dove deep into the busy-ness of life. I worked full-time, I went back to school to obtain my master's degree, and then I earned my Specialist Degree in Education. I kept myself busy by loving God, spending time in prayer, loving my children, and I loved serving the children at my former church. I wrote plays and I was in charge of programs at the church. You name it, I did it: Black history, Christmas, Easter, and Vacation Bible Study. All the busyness felt great at the time until I became overwhelmed and crashed.

I did not realize that I was loving everyone else but myself. I had no clue that the rejection I had experienced throughout my life had turned inward. Loving God, I was driven to keep moving to perform and to prove that I could make it. I felt like I had to stay busy because when I slowed down, I felt like I was a failure. This was a lie from the pit of hell. The truth is, slowing down to take things off my plate to care for myself, is a ministry unto God. Being extremely tired and worn out is not a testimony to God. I have realized that busyness is just a strong band-aid, but the antiseptic is God's healing truth. Somewhere down the line, I developed The Martha Complex. I thought that I had to stay busy performing, when I could have been flourishing by being kind to myself and spending time developing relationships, like Mary. Now, I realize that evolving personally and nurturing re-lationships is a ministry to God. This cycle of overwhelm had to be broken in Jesus' name. It took going through quarantine 2020 to realize the things that matter the most. Through slowing down, Father began to show me my family tree and how deeply the roots of rejection are planted. It is one thing to recognize the issue, but another to allow God to shine a light on the issue and come up with a strategy to cancel the generational curse. The tree of rejection has many branches that have affected my life in the following ways: low self-esteem/inferiority complex, fear of others' opinions, an inability to communicate, perfectionism, independence, pride, and self-rejection. God is still helping me put everything into perspective to silence the voice of rejection. This is a journey, and with God, all things are possible for those who believe.

It is amazing how powerful the word "perspective" is. I learned that people could look at one object or situation and have two different views about it. We usually decide something according to how we have been socialized. I had to pay close attention to what I was saying. After my first marriage, I made some negative vows that hindered me from being free to welcome a new love. I soon learned that I had to reprogram my mind, my words, and my expectations. I didn't have to allow the cycle of failed relationships to repeat itself. I had to learn to speak God's word with force to break the cycle of failed relationships in my family. I began to study God's word just like I was studying for a test. I researched scriptures that related to rejection and its rotten fruit. I had to remember that it is God's word that speaks louder than any rejection that I have encountered throughout my life. The voice of rejection was very loud, and it told me that I would never be married and that I would always be alone. I learned that God's voice is louder than any generational curse. I will not be alone for the rest of my life. I went to war using God's word and I did not waiver. God answered, according to my faith and my obedience. God's promises are, "yes and amen", and I am remarried.

Walking in freedom from rejection is a journey that should be taken daily. God's word helps us to see clearly. Rejection made me miss out on the beauty of people, places, and things because of my perception. Most importantly, I had also missed seeing my beauty and worth. I thank God for blessing me with a spiritual father, Apostle Lee Lyons, who helped remind me of my worth, validate me, and push me to soar in the realm of the spirit.

My father's rejection made a permanent imprint that will last for generations. Unfortunately, rejection was coded in my family's DNA. To make matters worse, when rejection comes, it never comes alone, but brings its entourage. I learned that rejection's ultimate goal is to cause isolation: mental, physical, and spiritual isolation. Looking back at my life, I recognize the times that I was rejected and my response. It is impossible to fulfill the Kingdom of God's mandate to build people up when dealing with issues of rejection. I decided to move beyond smiling through my pain. My desire for deliverance has become stronger than my desire to remain in dysfunction. Courage has led me to face rejection and dismantle every lie that it has told me. I decided to leave my comfort zone, the busyness and overwhelm, to come out of isolation and silence, to encourage others who may have had similar life experiences. I am victorious because God is my father and He signed my birth certificate by speaking of life in the beginning, and I am the apple of his eye. I am fearfully and wonderfully made. In Him, I am complete, lacking, and missing nothing. I am a Daddy's girl!!

Looking back, I am so grateful to my mother for being the essence of a strong Godly woman. Before I knew about the titles of "intercessor" and "prayer warrior" my mother taught me the fear of the Lord, and how to call on the name of Jesus. Yes, she was my first prayer coach. Now I understand that it was my mother's ability to pray and trust God that gave her the strength to keep pushing for better to raise her two children. I am so appreciative of my mother's tenacity and fortitude, as she was the only one out of ten siblings to graduate from college, and she did it all as a single mother.

We do not become who we are overnight. The fact is that life confronts us with generational patterns that desire conformity. Conformity is a dictator, and no one questions the way we think, feel, and do things. I am grateful to God because his truth silenced the loudness of rejection, victimization, and shame in my life and revealed his ultimate plan for acceptance into God's family, victory over every circumstance, and favor with God and man.

From brokenness to wholeness…from voiceless to victorious.

ABOUT THE AUTHOR

Tonya B. Clinton, Ed.S., is first and foremost a wife to Zerric Clinton, Ph.D., and mother to Edward, Makaya, Jasmine, and Andrew. She is affectionately called, "The Builder" as she purpose-fully builds fiery prophetic prayers for breakthroughs. Tonya uses her testimony to encourage those who have been broken and silenced by life's challenges to know that they are one word away from breaking out of old cycles through using the word of God and making victorious decrees.

Tonya is a certified Life Coach, Professional Educator, and Director of The Ablaze Girl Empowerment Program. She currently resides in McDonough, Georgia, with her husband and children.

CHAPTER 3

The Neighbor's House "Oh, Happy Day"

by Ynwanda Market

I remember when I was a young child growing up in a little town by the name of Hurtsboro, Alabama. It is a place where everyone knows everyone. The neighbor's house was the place where family, friends, laughter, and fun always resided, until one moment in time would change my outlook of the neighbor's house and my life forever.

Just to give a little back history, my biological mother was adopted as a baby by a beautiful couple that did not have children of their own. When my mother became pregnant with me as a teenager, it was my grandparents, Lizzie and L.K. Market, whom I called

Mama and Daddy, that would bring me home from the hospital and raised me as their own. Mama and Daddy had raised my mom and were now raising me. I was the only child at home with Mama and Daddy after my mom moved away until years later, my brother would come to live with us as well. Mama and Daddy were my everything. Mama was a homemaker, while Daddy worked. They made sure that I had everything that I needed and a little bit of what I wanted. Mama was a light-skinned lady, stout, not very tall, but not so short either. She always kept her shoulder-length salt and pepper hair curled with pink rollers. She was not fancy, but she liked things to be nice. Mama was the type of person that was very outspoken with a big heart. She did not play any games and was the disciplinarian in the house. Yep, we got whippings, done with so much love (laugh out loud). Back then I would say Mama was very strict, but now I realize that she was very structured and taught morals and values. The neighborhood kids thought that she was so mean, but little did they know she was a big ole teddy bear. She would give you the shirt off her back and all the food on her table. Everyone in the neighborhood loved her and Daddy loved her so much. She loved to play cards with her card group and was an usher and deaconess at church. Daddy was a deacon and worked closely with the pastor, so as you can see, I was brought up in the church and spent many days and nights there. Mama was my best friend. She was the one who always showed me a lot of love, you know that unconditional love that you do not have to question. I was also her favorite too. I was so happy with just hanging out with Mama, her love was the most beautiful and amazing love any child could ask for or want. I could see the love she had for me in her eyes whenever I looked at her. She loved me from the pit of her soul, and it was expressed to me down to my soul. She would always love me in some way or another. Daddy would say that she allowed me to get away with things that he knew she would not allow anyone else to do. She would take me everywhere she went; I was glued to her leg. She called me her little black gal. I would always sit on Mama's lap every night and watch TV until I fell asleep. She taught me everything I needed to know to be productive in life. She was so soft and cozy that I loved to lay on Mama. I was always touching her. I enjoyed just sitting in her presence, the calmness, and just knowing that she was there was all that I needed. I always had to be near her. I slept in the bed with Mama every night, just being able to smell her scent was all I needed to sleep peacefully. She had a scent of joy that I loved to smell. I was one happy child. I needed Mama just as much as Mama needed me. We were our own Bonnie and Clyde, without the criminal acts. Mama always made sure that I knew God in my life, which I later found out was all I truly needed. Daddy was special, but Mama was so special, I can honestly say now that she was truly a gift from God sent to me, just for me. So, as you can see Mama was a very important and pivotal part of my life. The thought of her ever not being a part of my life was so far from my mind. I did not know what I would do without her.

Now Mama allowed me to have a few friends in the neighborhood, but there was one person I bonded with who became my childhood best friend. The neighbor's house, whose owners were named Mr. and Mrs. J, was about three houses down the road from my house. They were known in the neighborhood by everyone and were friends with Mama and Daddy. We all attended church together and it was the village that raised each child that lived there. I was about four or five as far as I can remember, and my best friend who lived in Connecticut would come and visit at the neighbor's house every summer. She was related to Mr. and Mrs. J which is how we met and became such close friends. There were two things that I always looked forward to each summer, going swimming at Holy Trinity during the week for Vacation Bible School, and my best friend coming to visit from Connecticut. When it was close to the time for her to come to visit, I would sit on the porch and look for an unfamiliar car, watching all the cars that came and went to the neighbor's house. Or, if I rode to the store with Mama and Daddy, I would look at the license plates of the cars at the neighbor's house until I saw that Connecticut license plate. I would know then that my best friend was in town. When I knew she had arrived my heart would beat so fast and my eyes would light up like stars. I would be so excited, jumping up and down like I was on a trampoline, I could not sit still, just back and forth all over the house waiting for the moment that we could see each other. I would make sure that I had completed all my chores and got ready so that I would not have any reason not to be able to go to the neighbor's house with my best friend. Those times when my best friend was there, we would have so much fun and I would often spend the night at the neighbor's house with her. We would play and talk and stay up late. We ate sweets, had good dinners and walked back and forth from the neighbor's house to my house all day long. It was a time that was filled with so much happiness and laughter. We spent a lot of time with her and her family and these special times would go on each year for many years. These were the happiest times of my life, but one day at the neighbor's house something happened that would change the direction of my life forever. A once-happy little girl would become lost.

Complicated Grief

"Grief never ends, but it changes. It is a passage, not a place to stay. Grief is not a sign of weakness, nor a lack of faith. It is the price of love." Author Unknown

According to Psychology Today, *"grief is defined as the acute pain that accompanies loss. Grief goes through stages. For some people, grief can be short term. But other individuals may experience prolonged grief also known as complicated grief, lasting months or years."* (www.psychologytoday.com)

Around the time I was eleven, turning twelve, Mama's health shifted and she started to experience more health issues that led to her being hospitalized. I then had to utilize all that Mama had taught me over my life so that I could take care of her at home. Mama would eventually become so sick that she could not get out of bed by herself, bathe, or do anything that she used to. Of course, Daddy was there to help Mama as well, but because she was my best friend, how could I stand around and do nothing? I remember the day that Mama got an infection and the doctors could not get it under control. Where I lived, the doctor would still make house calls but she said that she would have to send Mama to the hospital. Anytime Mama would go to the hospital I was always allowed to go and visit her until she came home. Not this time. When they took Mama to the hospital, I stayed at the neighbor's house. I could not understand why I couldn't visit her this time. My mama was very sick. I will never forget an evening in September of 1990 when I was at the neighbor's house, the place where all the happiness and fun resonated, the place of laughter, and family times together. I was sitting and waiting for someone to come and take me to see my mama at the hospital. I was a kid so I didn't know what to expect, but instead, the neighbor's phone rang. When she answered it, there was a pit in my chest that until this day I can't explain but I knew, something wasn't right. On the other end of the phone was Mama's daughter. Whatever was said to the neighbor from the other end of the phone, from the look in her eyes I knew that something was not good with Mama. She had a look of calmness but sadness that she was trying to hide from me. I sat there in anticipation just waiting to hear what was being said on the phone. Then finally, she gave the phone to me and the first thing I remember saying as I put the phone to my ear was, "When will I get to come up there and see Mama?" I wanted to visit my mama. I was then told that Mama was no longer here anymore, she had gone to heaven to be with God. I could not believe it, I just kept saying, "But I need to see her." I needed to see for myself that I did not have a mama anymore. I begged for someone to please come and get me so that I could see Mama. I couldn't bring myself to believe that Mama had left me because she said that she would never leave me. She said that she would always be there with me, that she would see me grow up into an adult and have children. My mama was not supposed to leave me. I didn't get to say goodbye, give her a kiss, or anything. When she left in the ambulance from home, she didn't tell me that she wasn't coming back to get me. She left me alone, by myself. I couldn't believe it, my mama was gone and nobody would help me get to her! I sat there feeling helpless, abandoned, confused, lost, and quite possibly a bunch of other emotions as well. I sat quietly at the neighbor's house with nothing to say but just felt so helpless. My body seemed to be cold and numb like ice. I felt that I had just been robbed of my best friend. I couldn't think. I didn't have the words to express what was going through my mind and body, because I could not understand. My sense of security was gone, I just could not imagine my life without my mama. At that very moment, my life as the happiest little girl in the world changed. I didn't know how I was going to make it through the rest of my life without Mama. I had no one to console me and to say that everything would be alright; no one to kiss the hurtful pain that my heart was experiencing and to say, "Do not worry, I have your back." I was alone in that corner at the neighbor's house. What was a 12-year-old kid supposed to do without her Mama, the one person that was all she ever needed? I never had the chance to see Mama again until it was time for the funeral. Losing my mama was the hardest thing that I had to endure and I was left with an empty void in my heart that could never be filled again and a useless life.

After losing Mama, I had to move in with my biological mother. This was a big transition for me because I did not want to go. I couldn't stay with Daddy because he didn't know how to take care of a young girl. I was all alone in a very big world with no one to talk to, no one to say everything was going to be alright, no one to wrap their arms around me and hold me, no one to help me process this new journey. I had never lived with my biological mother before, and she was not used to having me living with her. She always lived on her own doing as she pleased. Now we found ourselves in a situation that no one was prepared for, and we all had to try and adjust, the best we knew how.

Time passed and as I got older, I didn't realize that I had not dealt with losing Mama. I kind of just went on with what life had dealt me and suppressed the pain. I felt very alone, abandoned, trusted no one, was scared, and started to get a little out of control. At my mother's house, there was no structure, everyone did as they pleased. There was no accountability, and I did not have to answer to anyone. My mother worked in several jobs, so she was not home much. She made sure the bills were paid and we had food, which I am grateful for, but no real family time existed. At this point, it was just my younger brother and myself taking care of each other the best we could.

I had a boyfriend, and by the age of 14 years old, I became pregnant and had my first baby girl. I was pregnant again at the age of 17, with my second baby girl, and left high school in my senior year. I studied and passed my GED all in the same year. A couple of years later, I got married to my children's father. We had a lot of rough patches during our relationship. I had experienced being cheated on and hurt, and I, too, had cheated. I endured domestic abuse, anger, low self-esteem, lack of confidence, depression, and abandonment issues, amongst other things. I was in a situation with no structure or guidance, alone, and we were both two broken people trying to make it together. At the age of 23, I became pregnant with my son. The only love at this point that I was ever sure of was the love that I had for my babies and the love that they had for me. My stepson eventually came to live with us, and I accepted him and treated him no differently as if he was my child. I enjoyed having two girls and two boys that called me Mom. Although I love being a mother, because of the issues that I had never dealt with, I was not too good at being the best mother, but I did the best I could. However, tragedy would strike again.

It was April of 2002 and I took the kids to school each morning. On this particular morning, before Jeshaun got out of the car he said, and I will never forget, "Mama, I love you." and I replied, "I love you more and see you this evening when I get home." He was such a happy child. He was such a joy to have as a son. He never complained and just enjoyed being loved and giving love. He was smiling and waving as I pulled away. Later that day as I sat in class, I would get a phone call telling me that I needed to get to the hospital because my child had been in an accident. Once I arrived at the hospital, I found out Jeshaun had been hit by a car crossing the street on his bicycle. He was only six years old. He did not survive the trauma caused by the accident. Once again, I was left by the person I loved most. Death would strike once again in October 2002, taking Daddy home to be with the Lord. God had taken another love from me. At this point, all I could think was why? Why God do you want me to be so alone?

I couldn't handle all those trials and that same year, my husband and I separated and eventually divorced. I never went to Mama's, Daddy's, or Jeshaun's grave after either funeral again. In my mind, all I would do was relive my past over and over. I could not find my way to the present. I walked around with a broken heart suffering in silence for many, many years, and never spoke of how I felt because no one would understand. There were many days that I would ask God to come and take me away from this earth because I couldn't handle the pain. I just wanted to die. I was very disturbed and no relationship that I tried to be in, would work out. It was me against the world. I was hurting and there was no way to fix it. I had no one. At this point, what would a young lady do with all that she had been through? How did I live life instead of simply existing?

As I got older, I was never consistent and stable. Now I guess you might say well, you were brought up in the church so why did you not seek God? Trust me, I knew of God, that I should love God, and my mama taught me how to pray, but during all this time God was the farthest thing from my mind, and actually, I wasn't too happy with God at the time. For many years, God was not truly on my agenda. I would go to church here and there, make false promises to God to get what I wanted, but I didn't have a true relationship. Nah, that was not what I was looking for. I had experienced three major losses that played a significant part in my life; no goodbyes, no warnings, no last I love you, nothing, just gone like a quick breeze. God did not even allow me to be there to see each one take their last breath. I didn't know how to deal with all of this.

Over the next 25 years, I could not get my life on track. I would move forward a little but nothing so significant that I could say that I was happy with myself or my life. I would start things but never complete anything. I was in a battle with hating myself and felt that no one loved me either. I was not living, and I was not carrying out any purpose. I was a very troubled soul with a lot of emotional issues that I carried around for a long time. I didn't mind being around people at times, but as soon as they left my presence, I could not wait to go and isolate myself. I would become who people wanted me to be at that moment. I wore a mask that hid all my pain, it hid my true self, and I hid me from me. I did not want to live but God would not allow me to die. Deep down, I was hurting badly and my grief had turned into self-suffering.

Once Broken but Now Healed

"I Am Free to Be"

In my mind and heart, each day was a struggle to live. I had so much love to give to others, but my biggest weakness was that I wanted someone to truly love me back. I wanted to feel the love that Mama, Daddy, and Jeshaun had shown me, again, and I just could not fill the empty void that was left from their deaths. There was nothing that I could do to replace what I had lost.

During the last five years to the present, I began to get sick and tired of my life in this dark place. I got tired of being a victim instead of a victor. I began to take the little bit that I knew about God and cry out to him. I was not fully committed, but I started, so what did I have to lose? Nothing! I began to get back into going to church each Sunday. I started to open my Bible a few times, again. I would have mini conversations with God occasionally. However, there was this one time I *really* had a conversation with God that changed my life. This was my conversation with God: I told God that I was in so much pain, I was sick and tired of being sick and tired. I had experienced so much hurt throughout my life. Nobody loved me, everybody was against me. "Where are you? Why did you take the ones that truly loved me? Why have I experienced so much hurt? Why have you left me? Why can't I get my life together?" These were just some of the questions that I had for God. With all that I had experienced, I really could not tell that God loved me and I didn't feel it. I told God that I was experiencing hurt, rejection, lack of love, and defeat. "God, where are you? I have experienced more hurt than any one person should have to go through, so God, where are you? My heart is shattered into a million pieces, I am damaged so, where are you?" I looked in the mirror at myself and said, "God, where are you? Love. What is love? So much hurt, so much pain. God, where are you? You said that you would never leave me nor forsake me, but it is hard to see that truth through all this pain that I am feeling right now. God, where are you? I am so tired of all these emotions and I don't want to become the pain that causes me pain. I drive people away, I isolate myself. I have a big heart that just wants to give and receive love. So once again, where are you?" Then God said to me in a still, sweet, small voice, "I LOVE YOU." At that moment, I felt God wrap his arms around me, as my tears would not stop flowing. I cried so much, I had a headache.

God showed me one scripture that day and to this day, I have it on the homepage of my phone so I can look at it daily. *"The Lord is close to the brokenhearted; he rescues those whose spirits are crushed. The righteous person faces many troubles, but the Lord comes to the rescue each time."* Psalms 34:18-19 (NLT) I took that scripture and I tried it, I held God accountable to it and I began to see myself differently. It didn't happen all at once, but it happened. I had to want a change in my life. The first step was admitting that I was not alright. At that very moment, I learned that God was with me all the time even during my darkest times. I began to search God's love through his Word, and guess what? He truly loves me.

As I began to reflect on the love of Mama, Daddy, and Jeshaun, I realized that all of that was God's love from the beginning. They taught me lessons before their death. Mama and Daddy taught me morals and values that would take me a long way in life, and they introduced me to Jesus. Jeshaun taught how to love. I just needed to learn to apply all these things in life for myself. Mama was an earthly representation of the love that God had for me, and more. Daddy showed me what a provider and trust looked like, the same thing I see in God. Jeshaun showed me what God's love and character looked like; love and humility. None of their deaths were really in vain, I just couldn't see the big picture. God was the void that I had been searching for all these years. I desire to take my life back. I want to live on purpose and in my purpose now. I actively participate in groups, where I have love and have learned fasting, prayer, and so much about the love of God and more. I began to seek counseling because I needed someone to talk to and to assist in dealing with my issues. I am learning techniques in dealing with and overcoming my issues and writing happens to be the most important one.

My pastor gave a sermon on forgiveness and with the help of God I was ready to forgive, and I also sought God for forgiveness for myself. The greatest gift of all is that God has blessed me with not only a mentor but a Spiritual Mother that always lets me know how loved and beautiful I am. I started participating in church events and ministries which has been a tremendous help. I can now see the sunshine where a dark cloud once hung over me. I have three living children and six beautiful grandchildren, and that alone means that I am tremendously blessed. For the last 25 years or so, I have existed on earth yet never lived my life to the fullest potential that God has for me. Oh, but God's love, mercy, and grace have caused me to look at life differently. I used to cry from a place of hurt and anger, but now I cry from a place of sensitivity. God has caused my heart to become even more sensitive, especially to the hurt of other people. I am continually growing in God and working on becoming the best version of myself that I can be. My purpose is not for me, it is for others and I am going to walk it out, upright. I serve an awesome God. He is my Daddy, Mama, and everything I need!

This year, I made the jump and visited their gravesites. It was emotional but I felt a sense of relief and that I could finally allow Mama, Daddy, and Jeshaun to rest in peace. It is okay for me to miss them; it is okay for me to cry sometimes because I miss their presence. I will always remember and cherish the memories I have of each of them. They will always be loved in my heart. However, it is not okay for me to continue to be stuck and suffer in life. I am now free to be what God has called me to be, living my life on purpose and assisting others in making their lives beautiful as well.

"All praise to God, the Father of our Lord Jesus Christ. God is our merciful Father and the source of all comfort. He comforts us in all our trouble so that we can comfort others. When they are troubled, we will be able to give them the same comfort God has given us." 2 Corinthians 1: 3-4 (NLT)

ABOUT THE AUTHOR

 Ynwanda Market has spent numerous years as a Certified Nursing Assistant, providing direct patient care, and holding certifications in multiple states. She has earned an Associate of Applied Science Degree in Occupational Therapy Assistant from Brown Mackie College Atlanta, Georgia. Ynwanda is a member of the American Occupational Therapy Association (AOTA). She is also an advocate for the Alzheimer's Association. Alzheimer's and dementia are passionate causes in both her personal and professional experiences.

Ynwanda, through wisdom and counseling, has learned to use writing as a healing tool during her emotional journey. Writing has become a method of escape from all the trying times that she has encountered and continues to encounter. She loves to learn new skills and expand her expertise. Ynwanda believes that no situation will overtake her life as she knows that her life is not about her. She knows that her assigned mission in life is serving others, being the hands and feet of Jesus Christ.

She is mother to four beautiful children and Nana to six awesome grandchildren. She was born and raised in Alabama, and during her childhood, she moved to Columbus, Georgia where she attended Eddy Middle School and George Washington Carver High School. You can continue following and learning more about Ynwanda Market by visiting her website at

www.ynwandasmarket.com and
Facebook @authorynwandamarket.

CHAPTER 4

Who is the Girl in the Mirror?

by Michelle Hudson

As I stared in the mirror I wondered, who is that looking back at me? This person has curly hair, big brown eyes, and a sun-kissed complexion. Who was this girl in the mirror? My mother was a beautiful, white Italian-Irish, 5'3" woman with gorgeous long brown hair. My favorite cousin had big blue eyes, blonde hair, and burned easily with too much sun. So, who was I? I didn't look like my mom and I didn't look like my cousin. I don't know if I favored my father because I didn't know him. I had one phone call from him when I was about seven years old, and then nothing. Why would I care who I looked like or identified with? I should not have had to worry about who I was, but some family members treated me differently.

I learned early on that there were differences between me and my family. The texture of my hair, the color of my skin, and my features did not connect me to the people that I called family. It was very hard to be different in my family because I couldn't identify with anything or anyone.

I grew up in the projects in Hartford, Connecticut and I had to learn how to live being me. The projects were fun because I was a part of other families which made up for the absence in my family. We just lived. I didn't go to church unless someone in the building invited me, perhaps for Easter or Christmas. I know that I was baptized as a baby because there were pictures in a book to prove the event had taken place. We were Catholic on paper, and I say on paper because if there wasn't a special event to attend, we didn't go to church. I went from time to time because the service lasted for 45 minutes and then I could say I went to church, plus there was Holy Water so I felt that I had made good strides in trying to be a better person.

I am Italian, Irish, and Black, which was hard to be during the early 80s. Every time there was a holiday break I would go and stay with my nana. Oh, how I loved my nana. She was about 4'8" tall with a petite frame and silky grey hair, and she was feisty! You know, the small ones usually are. Her scent made me feel safe and Nana had a way of making me feel safe. My fondest memory is that she would make the best pancakes. Out of all the Italian dishes I could have thought of, I remember her pancakes. When Nana cooked for me, I felt special. I felt loved. She did the best she could to make me feel important and included.

Nana prayed. She would say her prayers during mealtimes and at bedtime, from what I saw. I remember there always being a Holy Bible on the coffee table and rosaries around the house. Oh, and how can I forget the big blue praying hands my mother made when she went to catholic school.

My mother had me when she was 18 years old. Looking back, I know she was not ready to be a mom because she liked to party. She was a single mom trapped in her sorrow and pain. She moved away from my nana after a traumatic time in her life and I was forced to grow up fast. My mother needed to find love. She was sad and always running into the next bad relationship. I felt like I was the mom because I cooked and cleaned as needed. You may say that is not a bad thing, but it depends on what you had to clean. Mom was a person that needed to have a boyfriend. At that time, she began dating someone who had four sons, one of whom I went to high school with. Things progressed quickly in that relationship and the next thing you know, she moved in with this man and his boys. His house was nice but I refused to live there. I couldn't see myself moving into someone else's house so I had to grow up! My mother helped me get an apartment and live on my own at 15 years old when I landed my first job at Popeyes.

A year passed and soon I was in 12th grade, my final year of high school. I had made it! My mother told me that she was pregnant and was going to have a baby. She had so much buried pain and she wouldn't speak about it, but now she wanted to talk. The mother I knew was strong and I saw her as my hero regardless of her choices. I loved her. Having a baby should be an exciting time, but instead, she also shared that she had cancer and was HIV positive. Mom found all this out by having an ultrasound for the pregnancy.

In the 90s, HIV was rampant and many people were dying from the disease. Was my mother going to die? This was a lot to think about! My mom was all I had in this world. She was my glue and no matter how dysfunctional things were over the years, and throughout her attempts to be a mom, she was my best friend. Over time, Mom left the boyfriend/father of her child and we moved in together so that I could help her with my little sister. I worked and supported my mother, so she and my sister didn't need anything. The baby's dad got very sick and eventually, he passed away. Within six months of his passing, my mom passed away too, at the young age of 42. My sister was four years old and I was pregnant with my first child. My mother passed two weeks before I gave birth to my son. I was devastated but at the same time, relieved, because mom suffered so much with her illness. Being left with a newborn and a four-year-old that has just lost both of her parents, flipped our worlds upside down. Everyone wanted to offer advice and tell me what to do as they were on the outside looking in.

I quickly became the center of attention because many people wanted to take my sister from me, for their own reasons, but if I had to guess, it was really because they didn't think that I could raise her. Honestly, I was afraid to raise her. She was a handful, but my mother made me promise her, in a dream right before she passed, that I would raise my sister and not let anyone adopt her. My mom was ill for many years before passing so she didn't have the opportunity to teach her what she needed to know. A four-year-old who had experienced so much loss was hard to watch. My little sis was angry. She lashed out, fought, and just shut down more and more as time passed. I was desperate to provide a stable family life for my sister and my son, so at the age of 24, a year after Mom passed, I got married.

Getting married gave me an instant family, something that I didn't have, because after Mom passed, my family as I knew them, all went their own way. Having help with my new, little, handsome baby and my sweet mini-sister was great. However, I wasn't ready for marriage and my independence kept me from being humble when I needed to be. This marriage came from a strong friendship that we had enjoyed for several years before we got married. As a couple, we did well. We had the house, the picket fence, the cars, the jobs, but my independence was very present in our relationship. It was a real struggle to feel that I did not have to do it all on my own and to allow someone to help me.

After five years of marriage, we divorced. Quickly, our one-time friendship had unpleasantly shifted, and I needed a new way, a new outlet, a new life. I stayed single for a little while until I met my current husband, Will. We hit it off instantly upon meeting and began dating. I enjoyed his energy and presence. He seemed to be interested in me and I needed that. Our relationship progressed quickly. We met in April and by August 1, I gave my notice to what I thought was my forever job and relocated to Georgia. I didn't know anything about Georgia and had no idea what to expect, but it had to be better than the drama-filled days that I was leaving behind in Connecticut. The only thing I did know was that leaving Connecticut meant leaving my pain, hurt, and memories there. However, I could not have been more wrong.

I rented a truck and packed up my whole life. Just like that, I picked up and took my sister and my son to begin our new life. By searching the internet, I secured a home to relocate to, in Georgia. One thing I knew for sure was that I am strong and a provider, and no matter what, we would be fine. I hoped to create a new life with new opportunities and to offer my children a home life that I had never had. Connecticut is expensive and if you want to give your family a safe place to live and a good education, well, it seemed nearly impossible, so I had to move.

Moving sounded like a good idea. My heart was in the right place. I truly wanted the best for my children, but my sister and my son were not happy. My son was only seven and little sis was 11 when we relocated to Georgia. I introduced them to someone that they didn't know and moved them to somewhere they didn't want to be because I needed a reset. This pattern was familiar from my childhood. I took my son from his father and his family, and my sister from her family on her father's side. I was stressed and I tried, but nothing ever seemed to be good enough. I started feeling that I was letting my family down.

After a couple of years of living in Georgia things were not working out for Will and me, so I moved out on my own. I needed a break. Could it be that I still had all this baggage that I had never really dealt with? Will was a private person and I was a communicator. I needed to know what was going on but I think that came across as me nagging. I noticed that I hadn't been on my own for a while and maybe I didn't know Will like I should or could. Will drew me in with his love for his mother. His big heart wanted to love and provide for me, but our timing seemed off. I liked him but when I moved to Georgia, I wasn't in love, I was in pain, with baggage.

Love grew over time. Our breakup was brief. I moved out in February 2005 and in May I became pregnant with a little girl. I was beyond excited. My little sister began to act out; maybe because I was having a baby or maybe because she just didn't want to live with me. I know the hurt and loss of our mom was hard and I know she held a lot in, as I did. She went to live with her brother in North Carolina to finish high school.

In December 2005, my daughter was born, five weeks early. She had to be here for Christmas. A few months later I began to hemorrhage, so I thought, only to find out that I was pregnant again. I found out when I was almost five months pregnant and this baby was born at seven months only weighing two pounds. What was I going to do now? There was no-one to help me. I was on my own to figure it out. My oldest son was a great help to me and did what he could every day with the babies. It was like having twins, "Irish twins" – two babies born in a calendar year. I felt like a single mother because Will was building a business that kept him from home quite often. As things got a little easier with the business, their dad stepped in and started to help me with the day-to-day responsibilities. He is the fun parent and one thing is for certain; he is a great father who loves his kids.

2013 was a year of many twists and turns. Out of the blue, I began to get dizzy. If I made the slightest tilt with my head or if I turned too swiftly, I felt sick or as if I were spinning. I was out a lot at parties and hung out until late hours frequently. I didn't even like to be out, but my boyfriend wasn't home, so I was lonely. I started having panic attacks every time I would get behind the wheel to drive. People prayed over me, but I didn't pray for me or accept their prayers as I didn't know how. I went to see a doctor but nothing helped. I felt like I was trapped and dying. I was afraid and didn't know what to do. My children's father thought I was being dramatic. Truth be told, I can be dramatic, but this was different. I had no control over this feeling. He felt like I was acting out for attention, but my pain was real and it was scary. I was diagnosed with vertigo and given some medicine to help with the symptoms, but nothing seemed to work.

By late 2014, I was still battling vertigo and working every day. It was a struggle just to get out of bed. My episodes were becoming more frequent and it pushed my baby daddy further and further away. I think he thought I was crazy. He began to speak to me less and I think he felt like I was making it all up. Who was I? Looking in the mirror, I once again did not recognize who I saw.

One day on the way to work, while I was at a stoplight, I cried out to God. I had never done that. Looking back, that wasn't even an option. However, on this day, it was a Monday at 7:45 a.m. in October 2014, I looked up and cried out to GOD that I could not do this; I didn't want to do this. I felt like I was dying and I was tired of fighting. I remember sweating and crying and ending up in the ER where they began to ask me questions. I answered as many as I could until I passed out. I showed signs of a mild heart attack and was blessed to make it to my destination the way I did. That was not me...that was God.

I stayed in the hospital a few days, and when I got home, my drama seemed real. I was shown some concern, if only for a moment. I found out by snooping, that my boyfriend was chatting with another woman they say don't look, because you will find. Little things here and there showed that I had been cheated on and it made me feel worse. I was broken. How had I let this happen? I needed help, but I didn't have anyone to turn to. If only my mother were there.

In a moment of grief I reached out to a childhood friend that lives in Georgia and she shared information about her church

with me because I had been looking for a church but had not
found one. At this point, I needed something because I felt in-
complete and was a mess.

In June 2015, I visited a church in Lawrenceville, GA, and it was
amazing. The pastor's sermon seemed like it was about me. How
did Pastor know? Who told the pastor about my past, my pain,
my loss? The message on that day was about bondage. What in
the world was bondage? I would soon find out. I started going
to the church regularly, and then I joined it. A call was made
at the end of a service and without pause, I joined this church.
I had never joined a church, let alone been consistent with attendance. I wanted to get involved so I looked for a group that
I could join because I was hungry for the Word and hungry to
learn more about God. I didn't have a relationship with God
at that time. I knew there is a God, I knew the love I have for
God, but I knew what I knew by words, not by my own heart.
I wanted a relationship.

On October 27, 2015, my daughter and I were baptized. Oh my,
that was such a beautiful day! I walked into the sanctuary after being baptized and the pastor was preaching about God not
giving us the spirit of fear. He presented an illustration of something that had made his mind fearful and that took over him
until he claimed the promises of our Father, and then the song
"Rise Up" was played. I cannot express to you the feeling that
came over me with that sermon and that song.

Was I living in fear? Fear of what? I thought I cannot be in fear, I
am not afraid of anything. Shoot, I am strong. All I knew was that
it had been almost five years since I drove my car on the highway
because of the dizziness known as vertigo and the panic attacks

that had consumed me. I worked in Sandy Springs and I would drive there on the city streets rather than the highway. It was safer for me because if I had an attack I would be prepared. I was never late. I just packed snacks and went on my way. That was Fear. No-one liked to ride with me! After church service one Sunday, Monday morning arrived, and it was time to get the day rolling. I had to be at work by 9:00 a.m. so I left at 6:30 a.m. to make my way. As I drove down the street, the road forked and pushed me onto the 316 which is a two-lane highway that I had avoided for the last five years. Shockingly, I was now on that highway! Suddenly, I began to hear the voices: you can't do that, you are nothing, you are a failure, and you are afraid. I rolled down the windows and yelled, "Get out of my car!" God did not give me the spirit of fear, but a spirit of SOUND mind, power and love (2 Timothy 1:7). I was quoting scripture. I had never quoted scripture but I now felt God's presence, his warm presence giving me the strength I needed to fight. In seconds, the energy shifted and just like that, the Holy Spirit removed those feelings! I was on fire. I wanted more. I drove and drove it was amazing! I noticed my life was changing.

In 2016, I started attending church on Wednesdays and would not miss a Sunday. I was reading the Bible on my own, which I had never done before. I was free as I was starting to understand what this bondage was all about. For years I hid my pain. I was abused, used, betrayed, angry, and I was living in sin. I had two children with a man I was living with and we were not married. At one time I had wanted to be married, and I was, but it wasn't because of love, it was because of my desire for stability, so the next time, it had to be because of love.

How do you recover from a pain so deep? How could I marry someone that I am not sure why we are together? We spent many years just being parents, and there was no romance, only love for the children. I was hurt, angry, and I wanted out. I told God I wanted out. You know how they say, "You want to hear God laugh…tell him your plan?" I didn't just walk away though. In the past, I would just leave and never look back but this time, I prayed to God for the answer. I had already taken the road that hurt my son, so I did not want to repeat myself.

This time, I was going to try something new. I asked the Father for answers because I was not alone and I had all I needed in God. I wanted him to give me the answer I wanted to hear, like yes, you go and go now. But he did not. Instead, I kept hearing, "Be still." I kept hearing, "You need to be married by the end of this year." This year…no, that was absolutely impossible! I didn't even like the man at this point, and I know he didn't like me either, so that was not going to happen. All I could think about was all the anger that people had caused me. My life was like an upside-down mess and it was not fair. Not FAIR, imagine that!

On April 13, 2016, and I remember it as if it were yesterday, we had a week-long church revival. On Monday, the first day, I couldn't wait to get out of work to get there. Will and I had a major fight because I wanted to go to church. Who argues about wanting to go to church? I was driving home, and he was telling me that because I was out of the house too much, I had his kids in the street. I am a fighter and I was ready to fight. Who is he to tell me what or where I am going, I thought? I was driving on the highway from Marietta in the pouring rain, crying and screaming at him on the phone when the phone went dead.

God told me to be QUIET. I heard it loud. He said, "QUIET and go home." But me, I wanted to fight. I pulled up to the house and Will was getting in his car. He is also one that likes to have the last word, but he got in the car and drove off. I walked into the house and it was as if I was having an out-of-body experience. I remember seeing my kids, who looked afraid, as I crawled to my room on the second level, with tears flowing. I went into the bathroom and I cried hard. I saw myself on the floor. I was sitting on the sink, watching myself. My children called my friend who lived two houses over because they could not get me off the floor. She laid over me in a turtle formation and prayed the entire time. I could hear my friend, not asking any questions, just praying. I had read about turtle formation in a women's group bible study that I was attending and here it was now, in the flesh. When I woke up, I thought it was 15 or 20 minutes later but it had been two and a half hours. She had put the kids to bed and when I got into bed, I felt light. Amidst my tears, I heard God say, "Let go, I got this. Stop being so proud. You are forgiven and you need to forgive."

The next morning, on April 14, 2016, my birthday, I awoke and looked out with one eye. Am I dead? Am I dreaming? Did last night happen? Will had come home, as he worked from 9:00 p.m. to 6:00 a.m., and as I headed out the door to go to work, he pulled up. I didn't know how to feel. Was this round two? What now, do I wait? The kids got in the car as he called my name. "YES," I responded. He said, "Happy Birthday. We can celebrate your birthday this weekend so you can attend the revival because I know that it is important to you." Wait! What? Who is he? I walked away. Immediately, the Holy Spirit spoke to me. It told me to look in the mirror. Who do I see? Is she flawed? Is she perfect? Does her attitude need to be adjusted? Really, God, I was trying to help you out. I found out real quick that God does not need my help.

Things started to get better and I shared with my boyfriend that God said we need to be married this year and we were already in April. He quickly let me know that was not going to happen, so I said, "If it doesn't, I am going to have to leave you." I didn't think I needed to be married until I was convicted of living in sin. I now felt that it was time for me to do right by God.

Late in August of 2016, our relationship progressed. We were finally starting to like one another again and things were good. We began dating and discovered that we liked playing kickball together so we joined a kickball league that plays on Wednesday evenings. After the game, he would rush off to work and I would rush home to get the kids ready for school.

The Moment You Never Prepare For

On Thursday, September 1, 2016, I was doing my daily devotion and preparing my mind for a new day. It was about 5:30 a.m. when my phone rang and it was a number that I didn't know. I answered the phone and a lady identified as a church chaplain asked if I was Michelle. When I said yes, she replied, "Your husband has been shot. You need to get to the hospital as soon as possible." Was this real? I was in shock when the phone rang again. This time it was his mother, confirming the call. The kids were sleeping in so I shouted their names and they came to the stairs, angry that I woke them. I blurted out, "Your dad has been shot, we have to go." My son immediately started screaming and crying which made me even more emotional, but my daughter said, "STOP! Get it together. Daddy will be fine, God's got this."

As I rushed to the hospital, my mind was racing. We found out that he had been shot eight times. As I was the girlfriend/baby mama, they would not share everything until his father, my children's grandfather, arrived. When he did we were told that Will had been ambushed by a resident at the hotel where he worked for six years. Everyone there prayed. I prayed, I begged, and I pleaded with God. I promised God that I would surrender if he would save my children's father. Will was on life support for two months and had over 19 surgeries. I lost my job because I needed to be by his bedside.

After several weeks of craziness, he opened his eyes. After all those times I had told him to shut up or didn't want to hear him, I was craving the sound of his voice. He couldn't speak for a few days, but the first thing he said was that he loved God and he accepted God as his personal savior. He told us that on the day that he was shot eight times, the shooter held the gun to his head, and Will cried out, "I have kids!" and the shooter continued to point the gun. Before he could pull the trigger, Will asked God for the forgiveness of his sins and asked Him into his life. The man pulled the trigger but there were no more bullets. The next thing Will said was that he forgave the person that shot him, and he finally asked me, "Will you marry me?"

Will stayed in the hospital for three months and I slept on the couch by his bedside. He was released on December 1, 2016, and we were married on December 31, 2016. I got married to my best friend, the same friend I had been running from for all those years, and the same friend I had expected to be perfect and without faults because I was. HA! I realized who I was and I realized my worth and our worth together. A small host of family and close friends surrounded us to support our union and our decision to make ourselves one.

On January 31, 2017, we were at church and there was a visiting pastor that came to prophesy over people in the congregation. The pastor had all married couples stand and asked how long they had been married. When we answered 30 days, the pastor said, "Your family was cursed and now the curse is broken. No matter what you face, you will now face it equally yoked, and God will bring you through no matter what the circumstance is."

As time progressed, my husband was getting stronger so I could get a job. We were very blessed to have so many people be there for us in our time of need. The love that was shown to us was such a blessing and covered every financial need we had. I was able to find a job, but our expenses were too much for the salary I was earning. Before Will was shot, we were going to purchase our home, but we were evicted and found ourselves homeless, which was devastating. However, we were now ready for this challenge and we were not defeated. We had a new strategy, we had God.

I shared my story because throughout my life I always wondered why things happen and while I still do not have the exact answers, I know that there is a purpose. I was quick to blame my hurt on my experiences, but looking back, it was me repeating a familiar cycle. I know now that I do not have to repeat such cycles. I know now about curses and releasing them from your life and the life of your family. I know now that our steps are ordered. God was preparing me and my children to be ready for war. I could not have endured without Faith and Belief. I am a better person today. I stopped looking at everyone else and I hold up my own mirror. For years I did not like that person and my choices were often a reflection of hurt and pain. Today, I am so blessed to say that girl in the mirror is humble and thankful for the trials that continue to make me stronger. Doors continue to open. I was blessed by God in so many ways including the completion of my degree and landing my current job. I know this was the work of the Lord and I am so grateful that His hand is on our life. We are a praying family and God put us together for a purpose. Will and I both serve in the church as willing servants of God, together, as a family.

ABOUT THE AUTHOR

Michelle Hudson calls Bridgeport, Connecticut home, although she has lived in the Metro Atlanta area since 2003. Upon her arrival in Georgia, she discovered a love for working in the education field as a Financial Aid Administrator. Michelle has always loved working with people and is recognized for her natural ability to make connections. She desires to always share her willingness to be a vessel for someone and to assist them with their educational journey and financial aid needs for school.

Michelle received her bachelor's degree in Business from the University of Phoenix and is currently working on a master's degree in Organizational Psychology. She enjoys participating in her church as a volunteer and giving back to the community, including her own foundation Hudson, Hope & Faith. The Hudson, Hope & Faith program was designed to support families in need during the holidays. This foundation was founded by Michelle and her husband, William after they experienced a tragic shift in their lives and overcame the odds, and they hope to be someone else's light in a time of need.

CHAPTER 5

Karma is a B**** Named Abuse

by LaQuanda Plantt

I started work at Wildfire Steakhouse in October 2006. It was a new restaurant, built from the ground up. I had my interviews inside Perimeter Mall at a table outside of Dillard's. They didn't have offices and once we started training, construction was still underway. When you open a new restaurant, you spend a lot of time in training because you learn the ins and outs of everything that has to do with the corporation that the restaurant is a part of. Corporate trainers are there to train and it is a very intense process. I would compare it to any college course, squeezed into four to six weeks. When you spend that much time training with a group of people you become good friends, and the group I trained with became family.

There were two departments at Wildfire Steakhouse. The front of the house consisted of servers, bartenders, hosts, bussers (server assistants), and management. The back of the house included all the kitchen staff and managers. The training was separate for the two departments. In restaurants, it is not uncommon for the kitchen staff to flirt with the servers. Years prior, that was how I met my husband, now my ex-husband. Let us call him Jay. Jay and I worked together at a New York-style steak house, Angelo & Maxie's, back in 2000. When I began working at Wildfire, I was married with two sons; my youngest was only six months old. Maybe after a month of being employed by Wildfire, one day the servers were walking into one of the private rooms towards the kitchen, which meant we had to pass the kitchen staff. Wildfire had an open kitchen so we could see the cooks worked. While passing the grill side of the kitchen, one of the chefs, called QB, asked, "You hungry?" Because I don't turn down food, I replied, "Yep," and he said, "Let me make you a 'leave your husband sandwich'." QB seemed like a nice guy so I let him make that sandwich for me. I wasn't attracted to him, initially, but we became good friends. We talked a lot. We would sit after work and just chat about work. I wasn't extremely happy at home so the attention was nice. Jay, at the time, didn't pay too much attention to me and we didn't do anything but work, so I was bored. It was refreshing to be able to just talk to someone who seemed to be on the same page as I was. QB was extremely ambitious, talking about his dreams and aspirations, and that was what attracted him to me. I admired that. I wasn't physically attracted to QB and although he wasn't ugly, he wasn't fine either.

My husband was then in his late 30s and he wanted to rap. He didn't want to learn the business, he just wanted to rap. Jay worked as a chef as well for many years but never wanted a promotion because that would get in the way of his music career. Years later, I realized I did the same thing for my film career but at the time, I didn't see that. I saw a father of four kids without a plan B. My husband was indeed good to me. He didn't abuse me or cheat on me (that I knew of), he just lacked ambition. I was unhappy in the marriage for a while and attended family counseling by myself because Jay didn't think we needed it, and I was the one who wasn't happy.

We met when I was twenty years old, started dating, and I got pregnant with our first son four months later. He already had two sons from a previous marriage, therefore, I knew he was a good father, so I decided to keep the baby. I got sick six months into the pregnancy and had to stop working so I was going to move back home to Connecticut. Jay didn't want me to move and asked me to move in with him. I had the better apartment so, initially, I didn't want to move into his place. The apartment complex was old, looked like it should have been condemned years ago, and I just didn't like it. I lived in a one-bedroom loft but because my rent was more expensive and he was footing all the bills, I moved into his place. I didn't work anymore – just stayed home barefoot and pregnant…literally. I attended doctor's appointments by myself because Jay always had to work. I didn't have a car and couldn't drive a stick shift (which is what he drove) so I took the bus to my appointments. That was the only time I left the house.

After J'von was born on October 13, 2001, we filled out the paperwork for the birth certificate and Jay wrote his birthday as July 27, 1969. I was born on October 8, 1979, so that was a ten-year difference. I looked at him and said, "This is a legal document, you can't lie on this!" Now I know you are wondering how the hell I could have been in the hospital, just having had this man's baby, and I didn't know his age. Jay looked young for his age, as do I, so I just assumed he was maybe 25. I asked him how old he was and he would joke and say, "I'm as old as the stars and moon in the sky," but he never gave me a number. When we moved in together, we celebrated his birthday the July before J'von was born and I used a question mark candle in the cake. Sadly, I was young, and I just didn't question it, but I never thought he was a decade older than me. That was the worst thing ever and I didn't talk to Jay for two days after that, but I did have his baby, so I forgave him, and we went home.

Jay was a great father. He took the first week that J'von was born, off work, to stay home and help me get settled with our new baby. We took shifts feeding and changing him and when Jay went back to work, he would make sure to feed J'von before he left so that I could sleep in. We got married in 2005 and had Jalen in 2006. Jay was the same type of hands-on father with Jalen. He picked up a second job delivering papers for The Atlanta Journal-Constitution and therefore, would have to wake up before 4:00 a.m. because he would deliver the papers to the stores and then head to his regular job by 8:00 a.m. He would feed and change Jalen before he left. I was lucky as he did what most dads didn't do and although he was a great dad, he was just an alright husband. After he lied to me about his age, I think the standards I had for him changed. I felt he should be further along in life, both financially and mentally.

In seven years there was never any progression. We never bought a home or a better car. We never took any vacations, other than when we went to his home in Hilton Head Island, South Carolina. I like Hilton Head, it is a beautiful place, but we didn't go to the vacation spots, just his family's homes. Another thing that annoyed me was that Jay was very dependent on his older brother Vincent. Vincent paid for everything when we visited Hilton Head. If I wanted to go out to dinner, we had to see what Vincent wanted to do. Don't get me wrong, I loved my brother-in-law! He always treated me very well, made me feel like family, and was the only member of Jay's immediate family to attend our wedding. However, I wanted my husband to lead us, but he didn't. We were opposites to that effect. I could be prideful, and he considered himself the "baby boy" and that his family should do things for him, especially after his mother passed away when he was 19. Almost two decades after her death, he still expected to be taken care of. I didn't like that and wanted a husband that took charge and made moves on his own. He didn't even take me on a honeymoon after we got married. Towards the end, he said we always had our bills paid and we had a place to live, which was true, but we didn't enjoy life together. That's what was missing. I met Jay when I was young, but as I got older, I wanted more. I wasn't sure what that "more" was but I yearned for it.

One night in December 2006, I was sitting in the car with QB talking and he asked if I wanted to hang out with him and play pool. I never did much other than work, so I was like, sure. That was the beginning of our affair. I remember the first time I cheated on my husband with QB, it wasn't even good, and I was mad at myself for breaking my vows for bad sex. I continued secretly seeing QB though, as I enjoyed our talks and his company, and I liked him. I thought QB was who I was supposed to be with and told Jay I was leaving him. It was the worst mistake I ever made. Not leaving my husband, because I was going to do that eventually, but the way I did it. If I could go back in time, there is one thing I would change…not eating that damn "leave your husband" sandwich. It wasn't even that good. It was a dry grilled chicken sandwich! I should have ignored QB after that.

Once Jay and I separated, I moved in with QB for a few weeks until my apartment was ready to move into. The experience wasn't horrible, but it wasn't great either. QB would go out a lot and didn't invite me to go. He would just leave me at his place alone. Once I moved into my place, he continued going out to parties, etc., without me. I was a homebody so it didn't bother me, but it was something I noticed.

During that summer, in July 2007, QB took me to Decatur, Georgia where his grandmother lived, to watch the fireworks. I met his mother there as well. She was a nice lady and I enjoyed meeting both his mom and grandmother and thought he must really love me to introduce me to them. Shortly after that meeting, QB's mother was diagnosed with cancer. I remember one morning as we were headed to his job (I would ride with him to work and jump on the train from his job to go to school, and then after school or work, I would meet him back at his job and we would ride home…that was our routine), his mom called and she was in excruciating pain. She was home alone, and she was on the floor in pain. QB was wondering where his dad was and frankly so was I, and I wasn't fond of his father after that day. I didn't understand what type of person would leave their dying wife home alone. QB was unsure what to do as I was with him and we were on our way to school and work. I had to yell some sense into him, "WHAT ARE YOU DOING?! GO TO YOUR MOTHER NOW! We can be late, I'm alright, your mother needs you, so go!" We drove over and he went inside to check on his mother as I waited in the car. He never invited me in. Never, ever, to this day, have I been in his parent's house. His mother passed away shortly after that.

I wasn't happy with the relationship, but I stayed because I wanted to be supportive. I felt he was in a bad space and I should stick it out because he was sad. Unfortunately, it wasn't just a phase. It was really who he was. He spent our first Thanksgiving with one of his "friends" that happened to be a female. QB had a lot of friends, all of them female, and all I believe he was sleeping with or had slept with at one point. We would argue quite often. I don't know why I stayed. We would break up and get back together. It was a cycle. We did that for almost two years and then I finally broke up with him. In January 2008, the day President Obama was inducted into office, we broke up.

Shortly after our breakup, I started dating a very nice guy who completely spoiled me. Let's call him, "Nice Guy." We went out on dates, he brought me gifts and was just a sweetheart. The only negative thing about him was that he was eight years my junior. QB started stalking me after I started dating Nice Guy. He would peep in my windows and lay on my patio in the wintertime waiting for me to get home. One night Nice Guy and I were in my room watching TV and I could see a shadow at my window. Nice Guy went outside and confronted QB. They exchanged words as QB kept his distance. It was obvious that QB didn't want a physical altercation with Nice Guy so he just blurted out insults. "You're not even her type. She doesn't like big guys," or something childish like that. Nice Guy came back inside and QB left, but not indefinitely. Shortly after that incident, Nice Guy and I attended a play and once we returned to my place, he kissed me goodbye and left. Minutes later, there was a knock on my door and I opened it thinking it was Nice Guy. QB burst through the door and pushed me down and snatched the necklace I was wearing from my neck. It all happened so fast that it was a blur. He was yelling over me as I was still on the floor from when he pushed me. There was an iron plugged nearby and he grabbed it and held it over me like he was going to burn me with it. I finally managed to get up and I ran into my bathroom and locked the door. I stayed there until he left.

Before that happened, I had called the police on several occasions, but they didn't do anything about him stalking me because he hadn't physically harmed me. This time, I finally had bruises, and although it's sad to say finally like it was a good thing, it was enough to show a judge. I took pictures, brought them down to DeKalb County Courthouse, and got a judge to grant me a restraining order. I thought the restraining order would keep me safe but it did not. I took the day off work to go to court for this restraining order and QB wasn't there. I sat and waited, only to find out he was never served the papers. I was devastated! I gave them his contact information including his home and work address and in the weeks before the court date, they couldn't manage to serve him?! I was convinced that the system wasn't going to do anything until he killed me. I lived in a gated community but QB always managed to get through the gate. I was afraid in my own home. I complained to the property manager but she stated there was nothing they could do to control him from coming onto the property. Someone was letting him in and there was nothing they could do. I was terrified so I decided to break my lease and move. The night I was gathering all my things out of my apartment, I saw QB near my unit wearing a black hoodie, hiding in the bushes. I called the police. This is how that went…

Me: My ex is outside my apartment. He has been stalking me.
Officer: Has he harmed you physically?
Me: Not today, but he has in the past and I tried to get a restraining order.
Officer: You have a restraining order on him?

Me: He was never served the papers but he's outside my window. I can see him!

Officer: Ma'am, unless he physically touched you, there isn't anything we can do.

Me: But what if he kills me? I can't call back then!

Pissed off and scared, I hung up the phone.

After QB started stalking me, I kept my boys away, with their father, as I feared for their safety as well. He had never shown any anger towards them, but I did not trust him and wasn't taking any chances. I was alone. Fearfully, I sat in my empty apartment, looking out the window until I watched QB, in his black hoodie, run up the hill. I watched until I could no longer see him, then I dashed out the door, ran to my car, and left for a new beginning. So, I thought…

QB only worked at Wildfire for maybe four months; I stayed for five years. One night he came up to Wildfire, sat at the bar, and tried to give me a ring. Yes, a ring! We weren't even speaking! I was mad at him, as usual, and he brought me a ring and attempted to propose, while still sitting at the bar. He opened the ring box and I just walked away. This was before I moved to my new apartment and after I moved, I avoided all contact with him. One night he called up to the restaurant and asked if I was working. The manager on duty told him I was and he just hung up. My manager found me and told me I had a call but they just asked if I was working then hung up after he told them I was. I started freaking out! I'm pretty private – well, not now since I'm telling you all my business in this book – but at the time I was private and maybe even embarrassed, but no one knew about what I was going through with QB. I had to inform

my manager that he was stalking me. After we closed the restaurant, my manager walked me to my car. I was driving home
and although I didn't see anything specific because it was dark,
I felt as though I was being followed. I drove to my new apartment and once I got to the gate, the feeling of being followed
was strong, so when I drove through the gate, I passed my turn,
kept straight, and drove out the rear entrance of the complex.
I drove to the nearest QT gas station because most gas stations
were well lit. I parked at a pump and looked around. I didn't
see anyone. I waited for maybe ten minutes, then left. I thought
that it might have all been in my head, so I drove back home.

At the time, my sister and I lived in the same complex and she
was just two buildings down. She was having a get-together that
night so I went to her place instead of mine. I parked and was
walking to her building when QB pulled up beside me and said,
"I have some mail for you." It was junk mail; nothing of importance, nothing I needed or wanted. My intuition was right!
The bastard followed me home and now he knew where I lived.
This moment was pivotal for me. I was officially afraid for my
life. After that moment, I was scared all the time and constantly looked over my shoulder. Even today, I get nervous if a car is
driving behind me for too long. That moment he instilled a fear
in me that I still carry with me.

The police failed me, and I feared for my safety as well as my children's. Dummy me decided to try to be nice and be his friend.
If we were friends, he wouldn't hurt me. That's what dummy me
told myself. A toxic cycle began after that. Just the thought of
it makes me so mad at myself for being so weak and just plain
dumb. Six months passed and we started being "friends" again.
Then he would do something to hurt me and I would stop talking

to him. He would do something to help me when I was in a bad place financially, and I would be his friend again. Occasionally, we would sleep together but there was nothing on earth that would make me enjoy it. That is how much I disliked him. I was mentally imprisoned for over a decade. He would help me and then hurt me in some capacity. He never put his hands on me after I started to fight him back but it would always be something and most of the time, it involved other women. He verbally and emotionally abused me. My self-esteem was trash and that is the only explanation as to why I put up with it for as long as I did. I thought God was punishing me for cheating on my husband and I was mentally lost.

The QB cycle lasted over fourteen years. I do not know if I genuinely wanted to believe he was a good person, or that I feared him, but I forgave him repeatedly. He would do something cruel, then apologize, and I would forgive him. Typically, I do not like to stay mad for a long time but I would get frustrated at myself for not being strong enough to walk away. QB would tell me that no one cared about me but him. "Where are your so-called friends when you need help? I'm the only one here always helping you, 'cause I care about you and I love you." He was the only one helping me, so I believed him, for a very long time.

I was appreciative of his help as he would help me pay bills or my rent if I wasn't working. He would give me money because he never wanted me to be broke. In 2016, he randomly sent me money via Cash App and called it "Boyfriend #2 expenses" and thought it was funny. Let's rewind a bit to when QB was stalking me. He was not just stalking me in person. It took me five years to find out he was stalking me online. For years, I had a Facebook friend name Song Zu. Song Zu commented on my posts, liked them, and there was an interaction between us for years. Randomly, I had asked QB to use his computer (we were most likely on good terms then) and he said, "Sure, let me log out of what I am doing." Before this day, I did not know this about Facebook, but if you have multiple profiles they will all appear on your login page. QB didn't exit out of the login page and there it was like a slap in the face, three profiles. QB, looking like Mr. Nice Sheep, profile #2 was "Mario" which looked like a cooler version of him, wearing shades and dressed like he was headed to the club, and profile #3 was SONG ZU! Song (insert profanity here) Zu. I was so angry, but I didn't say one word, I just went into my account and blocked Song Zu. Since he is such a stalker, he noticed almost immediately and had the audacity to be mad that I blocked his fake stalker account in which he pretended to be an Asian female. I should have known better…Asians do not spell Song they would have used Sung or something like that. Either way, I should have known better, but I didn't. I am disappointed in myself for how I allowed him to treat me. I did not fully believe in myself or that I could survive alone when I hit a bump in the road. I thought that I needed to be rescued instead of figuring it out for myself. I didn't see what other people saw in me as I undervalued who I was as a person and needed constant reminders that I am LaQuanda Plantt, and that I could accomplish anything. I was not that LaQuanda Plantt yet. I still had to go through a little more pain before I got there. I had not had enough quite yet.

In July 2019, I won an award for Most Influential Casting Company (by this time I had been a Casting Director for almost a decade). That night as I wore my gown and gave my inspirational acceptance speech in front of family, friends, and a room full of strangers, I was facing eviction. I was unemployed and did not have a dime to my name. So, guess what I did? Yes, that is right, I called QB for help. Have you reached the point where you are yelling at me while reading this as we yell at stupid people on the television screen? "Girl, what are you doing?!"

After 14 years, one thing I know is that QB never helps because he actually loves me (insert a side-eye here) or cares, he does it for the control he wants to have over me. He will help but there will always be a catch. He became so predictable in his requests. I always knew they would have something to do with sexual intercourse and if I said no, he wouldn't help me. Never mind the money I borrowed to pay my rent during the eviction. We wrote an agreement that I had to pay him back, but QB being the wolf in sheep's clothing that he is, suggested in August that he help me to get a cheaper apartment. He said he did not mind helping me since I wasn't working but my rent was too expensive. My initial response was no because I did not want to be tied to him through a lease and I did not want to be in a relationship with him. He said we did not have to be in a relationship; he just wanted to help me (you can sigh here if you want to). QB helped me pay July's rent to prevent eviction because I still wasn't working.

All was well for a little while, meaning we were getting along. He brought up getting me another apartment again. I did not want to leave my current apartment as I enjoyed living there but truth be told, I could not afford to pay the rent, not working full-time. I finally agreed. I know what you may be thinking… Cry me a river. Some guy offered to get you an apartment. However, one thing I learned in this last year is that we all may be going through something. Someone may be going through something worse than you but that doesn't mean what you are going through is not important, or that it doesn't matter, as I used to think for many years. Here I was, receiving money, help with bills, free trips, etc. A lot of women would kill for that so I should be grateful. I just hated how he spoke to me and treated me so, at the end of it all, those other things did not matter to me. I was internally damaged. I knew in the depth of my soul this was not a good idea. Look at our track record. Nothing, and I mean nothing he has ever done for me has been with sincerely genuine intentions. Have you ever seen that movie Cruel Intentions where the sister was just so evil that everything she did had an ulterior motive? That is QB and I knew this. In my prayers, I knew it. I even spoke to Queen Mother, Chris Scott, about it and she advised me not to do it and to stay away from him. That is what I wanted to do but where was I going to go? Where would I live?

When I moved out of my apartment, I cried for days because I felt trapped. I needed a place to live but I seriously didn't trust him and even my best friend said to me, "Friend, I know you don't want to go with him and I wish I could afford to help you. It sucks 'cause it seems like it is your only option." Can you imagine the mental defeat one feels when they feel like they do not have any other option? Especially when children are involved? I will say I never allowed QB to spend too much time around my sons, so they never knew the type of guy he was.

The move-in date was in November 2019. Initially, he found a place in October, but the leasing office messed up the paperwork and he told them he didn't want the apartment anymore. In that month, QB changed his mind several times depending on his mood. Seriously, one day he was helping me because I needed it, and the next day, he wasn't helping me because I wasn't his girlfriend. One week it changed every single day, four days straight.

The terms of him getting the apartment, says him, was that he wanted a copy of the key because he wanted to come and go as he pleased and have access to me, but I had to pay all the rent. Say what now? You want a key, you say? Come and go as you please and I have to be your beck and call girl? No, sir.

Once I moved in, I sent an email thanking him for everything. I expressed how much I appreciated him helping the boys and me with a place to stay but as of that day, we would no longer be intimate. I made it clear that he could no longer use my body as his play toy. We could be cordial but I was no longer willing to sleep with him. Let us just say that did not go over too well and for the next nine months, QB made my time in that apartment hell on Earth. Even though I paid the rent, he put the gate code in his number so that people had to call him to get in the gate. He did not put my email on the portal, so I had to send the rent money to him every month. For me, everything should have been fine. I was paying the rent and I did not have male company over but that didn't stop him from constantly harassing me and threatening to kick me out every other week, all because I would not sleep with him. This man was causing all this drama and he had a girlfriend that was living with him. WHAT?!?!

He was doing all sorts of things to me, treating me as less than trash, forcing himself on me, and he had a live-in girlfriend. She was smart too. She went through his phone one day, found out about the apartment, and left him. He blamed me for that, of course. That man never took any accountability for his actions, as he was a pure narcissist. I was in the apartment for four months and then COVID happened. I was out of work, I had not received any unemployment benefits, and I had no idea what I would do. QB took this opportunity to drag me through more emotional hell. Let's be clear, QB is NEVER worried about money. Anytime he wants to fix something, he throws money at it and thinks all is well. He paid the rent when I could not, but he put me in a bad place where I truly believed I was depressed. QB would spend hours calling or texting me from different numbers. He had the locks changed multiple times, but the leasing office would always bring me the key. Then one day, he had the locks changed when I wasn't home, and the boys and I were locked out. The next day when I had to meet him to get the key (he kept one for himself), he said, "This is what I have to do to see you for the first time in 2020." After that, a few more incidents occurred but I can proudly say that my last straw was when I had to call the police on him for trying to force his way into the apartment while my boys were home alone. He called maintenance to break the door down, and I called the police and the police ordered him to leave. This fool had brought furniture as though he was moving in!

I knew that once he would do all that in front of my boys, I didn't want anything from him ever again, and after being in a pandemic for over five months with no income, I knew I never wanted to be in that financial predicament ever again either. Less than two weeks later I received the financial blessing I needed to leave that apartment and move into my own. As I write this, this is literally one of the proudest moments of my life as I moved days ago. I have shared my story as it was happening in real-time and I am blessed that I can end it with a happy ending!

ABOUT THE AUTHOR

LaQuanda Plantt, Casting Director, Filmmaker, and Life Coach founded ElleQ Casting in 2009 and ElleQ Productions and ElleQ Coaching in 2017. She has worked on numerous projects directed and produced by some of the best in the business, including Ava Duvernay, Oprah Winfrey, Adam Shankman, and Barry Jenkins. At the tender age of 14, LaQuanda wrote the award-winning essay, "What Black History Month Means to Me" which was inducted into the Congressional Record in March 1994 and twenty years later, she assisted with the casting on the Academy Award-winning film, Selma. She has cast and/or produced films that have aired on Amazon Prime, BET, Netflix, and Showtime. LaQuanda is a certified Life Coach, specializing in the entertainment industry. She recently began teaching and coaching actors and individuals interested in a film career.

Via ElleQ Casting workshops, social media, and guest speaking appearances, LaQuanda wants to encourage others that dreams are not limited. If you believe and work hard towards manifesting your beliefs, you can achieve anything you dream of.

"Nothing is more satisfying than assisting another person to fulfill their passion and live out their dreams."
- ElleQ

CHAPTER 6

What Don't Kill You Makes You Stronger

by Consuelo Allen

I was sitting on the third pew back from the front, second seat from the end, totally captivated by the sight of the tall, dark, and handsome young man that sat behind the five-piece Pearl Roadshow drum set. The sound he made with those drums… Every beat of the bass was mesmerizing, and I was hypnotized by the ringing of the high hat. Sunday after Sunday, I would sit in the same spot, in awe of the sound and sight. At 13 years old, I had fallen in love with a young man that was talented and very popular, not to mention five years older than me. He was a man that I knew would never choose me because I was too young and still had my innocence.

Our families sang together every Sunday at Consolation Baptist Church. After every program, I would find some reason to go over to start a conversation with him, or as best I could as a naïve 13-year-old. I never really had much to say. I would just stand there smiling so hard that my cheek muscles started to hurt. He would say to me, "Girl, you better go somewhere before you get yourself in trouble." However, I heard something different, "I like you, even if you're 13, you can still be my girlfriend." At a very young age, I was always determined and persistent, no matter how many times his father and mother would tell me to stay out of his face because I was too young. I was not going to stop until I got his attention.

Leaving the church, I said to my cousin, "One day, I am going to be his wife." We both liked him and would argue back and forth about who was going to be his wife. I would say, "I'm going to marry him," and my cousin would say, "No you're not, I'm going to marry him and we are going to have three kids and two dogs!" We were just kids that had a huge crush on Lorenzo, but for me, it was more than just a crush. I wanted him to like me the same way I liked him. I had to come up with a plan to get him to come to my house, so I could show him I was not just a little girl.

When the next Sunday arrived, I had to get prepared. I moisturized my jerry-curled hair and put on my perfume and lip gloss. I grabbed my blue slingback heels and blue and white dress out of the closet, the one my mom told me I couldn't wear it because it showed too much cleavage. We pulled up to the church and I walked down the middle aisle and sat in my usual spot. I glanced over in his direction, only to find him looking at me. My heart started pounding. I felt little butterflies in my stomach. I thought to myself, ok, I have his attention, now I have to make my move. After the program was over, I walked over to him and started making small talk. I looked out the corner of my eye and saw his drumsticks lying on the floor. It hit me! If I took his drumsticks, he would have to get them from the house. In my mind, that was a brilliant idea, seeing as though he lived on the next street over and he walked past my house every day after school. Some days he was with his girl-friend, but I didn't care. I refused to let her get in the way of me having the boy of my dreams. I grabbed the sticks, turned around, and walked away fast. He said, "Girl if you don't bring my sticks back!" I kept moving, shaking them in the air, and yelled back, "You know where I live."

By the next week, I wasn't sure if he would stop by the house, and in all honesty, I wasn't sure if I was ready for what could happen if he did! After a few days, the day I was anxiously awaiting, fi-nally came. I was sitting on the front porch after school, look-ing up the street, when I saw that tall chocolate boy with those sexy bowlegs walking toward me. I could have spotted him from a mile away. He got to my house, stopped in front of the stairs, and said, "Can I get my sticks?" I sat there smiling and giggling just like a little schoolgirl. I replied, "They're in the house. Let me go get them." He stopped me as I was getting up. "Better yet, I'll be back tomorrow, but I'm coming for more than my sticks." I thought to myself, OMG! What did he just say? What more is he coming for? Could he really be referring to what I think he is referring to? I pushed those scary little girl thoughts out of my head and responded, "Whatever, come back tomorrow. I will be here." I watched him walk away until he finally reached the alley-way that connected our streets. Then I jumped up and ran into the house to use the bathroom. The thought of what he meant by "more than my sticks" gave me the bubble guts!

I walked into my room, fell backward on my bed, and started contemplating. Was I really going to do this? All kinds of thoughts ran through my head, "You said you wanted to show him you are not a little girl. You are only 13 and he is 18. What is he going to do to me? Will it hurt? Will he like me afterward?" I placed my hands on my head to shake those thoughts away. The sound of my mother's keys coming in the back door was the only thing that snapped me out of my intense train of thought. I went to the kitchen to greet her with a hug and a kiss. "Will you be late again tomorrow?" I asked. (I was a latchkey kid after my parents divorced.) Her response was, "Yes baby, all this week. Will you be ok?" It was so surreal but tomorrow was going down! "Yes, mom I will be fine." (I hoped.)

After a full day of anticipatory anxiety, the time had finally come. When the doorbell rang, I was standing in the hallway with drumsticks in hand, looking at the door, knowing that once I opened the door, my life would change forever. A part of me hoped he would just take the sticks and go home. I opened the door slowly and invited him in. Looking up into his dreamy eyes, I nervously said, "Here's your sticks." He replied, "I told you if I came here, I'm taking more than my sticks." I was stuck; paralyzed with fear. I couldn't move. My heart started beating fast, I felt butterflies in my stomach, and my palms were sweaty. What had I gotten myself into? He walked over to me kiss me on the forehead and whispered in my ear, "Are you sure you are ready for this?" He led me over to the couch. After minutes that seemed like hours, my innocence was gone.

Days turned into months and months turned into a year of me being his little secret. Every other day he would stop by my house after school and I would allow him to have his way with me.

I knew what we were doing was wrong. I didn't know how to stop it. However, there was more to Lorenzo than met the eye. I didn't know that I wasn't his only secret.

Sundays would roll around and that was the only time I was able to see him outside of the afterschool hookups. One Sunday, my cousin and I walked into the church and it was extra crowded so we could not sit in our usual seats. We sat in the back of the church. Once we were seated, I started looking through the crowd for Lorenzo but didn't see him anywhere. I heard someone on the drums but realized that it wasn't him. When the program was finally over, I went over to his brother to ask where Lorenzo was. He replied, "I'm not supposed to talk about it, but he was arrested last night for possession of drugs and breaking and entering. My heart sank. I instantly felt sick as the news hit me like a ton of bricks. I could not believe what I had just heard.

As I sat in the back waiting for everyone to pack up, I felt so sad and confused, thinking to myself, how could this be? Drugs, burglary… Who would have ever thought? As I sat there, someone walked up to me and said, "Hello, I'm Akron, the guy on the drums. How are you? I noticed you noticing me. Have we met? Maybe not, but it's ok. Here's my number, call me anyway." I took his number to keep from being rude. Then my cousin came over to tell me what she heard about Lorenzo. "Did you hear Lorenzo was arrested? I heard he might be in big trouble." I dropped my head in disbelief.

I had become accustomed to our afterschool hookups. It was so difficult not hearing that doorbell ring after school. I found myself in a state of depression. My family knew I was sad, but they never knew the circumstances behind my sadness. I couldn't tell anyone about our secret because of our age difference. I did not want to get him into any more trouble. I finally had to tell my cousin, which was hard for me because she was such a good girl, who loved the Lord, and would never sin as I had. I didn't want her to judge me or think less of me. As I confided in her, she told me, "It's ok, God will forgive you. You just cannot behave like that anymore." It sounded so simple coming out her mouth. We all know that some things are easier said than done. Being so young and exposed to sex, I felt like this was something I was supposed to do. I had taken on a toxic mindset when it came to sex. In my mind, it was the only way anyone would like me.

My promiscuous behavior continued, causing me a lot of heartache and pain. Eventually, I grew tired of my behavior and decided I wanted something different. I remembered I had met a nice guy at church, who seemed to be different. I took a chance and gave him a call. My assumption was correct. He was so nice we would talk on the phone for hours every day. We started spending time together and he showed me what it was to have a real relationship. It felt nice to have someone that truly liked me for me and not just for sex. We decided that since I was only 14 and he was 18, we would not cross that line. We would go out, have fun, and just enjoy each other's company.

Things were going as planned until one Friday when his mom picked me up from school and we went to hang out at her house. His mom was the coolest person you ever wanted to meet, along with his two little sisters that I fell in love with the first day I met them. Everyone was excited that we were visiting but I didn't know that a one-day visit was going to turn into a full weekend.

The house was full of life and fun, with everyone playing cards, drinking, and talking loudly. This was all new to me, but I enjoyed the excitement. As the night ended, his mom said, "It is too late to take you home. I will call your mom to let her know I will bring you home tomorrow." She called my mom. My mom said, "No way are you staying over there. You are not grown." I started yelling, telling her how it was unfair (I was a spoiled brat, who always got her way), and she finally gave in and said it was ok. Really, it was not ok. Akron had been drinking, everyone was asleep, and as I laid in the bed with his little sister, I felt someone tugging at the comforter I was sleeping under. I woke up to him standing over me gesturing for me to follow him. Before I knew it, the line we vowed not to cross, was crossed!

That weekend soiree became a ritual. Weekend after weekend, I would leave school as a young lady and return home as what I thought was a grown woman. In reality, I was doing grown-up things, but I was not grown, but rather a little girl that was in over her head. Being so naive and oblivious, my reckless behavior had finally caught up with me. Suddenly, I was waking up every morning with a queasy feeling in the pit of my stomach, my jaws clamped tight, sweating profusely after every visit to the porcelain god. I thought to myself, why am I sick? What could it be? What did I eat? Then it hit me like a ton of bricks! I was not sick. I was 14 and pregnant! There were consequences for my actions.

The following week, my greatest fear was confirmed as a nurse handed me a slip of white paper with the words "positive" circled in red ink. As I sat there with tears falling from my eyes, I hung my head in shame. What now? How would I tell my mom? What would everyone say? I was a disgrace to my family.

During the ride home in the car, it was so silent, you could hear a pin drop. Finally, out of the silence rose Akron's voice, saying, "We are too young to be parents. We cannot have a baby. I am joining the army." I became so angry and felt betrayed. He did not even ask what I wanted or how I felt. It was all about him. Even though he was right, I didn't want to hear that from him.

We mustered up enough nerve to tell our parents and quickly concluded that having an abortion was the best thing to do. My mom and Akron took me to the clinic. It was the worst day of my life. We walked into the cold, dark, somber office and I sat in the waiting area shaking uncontrollably, waiting to hear them call my name. The door to the procedure room opened. "Consuelo Allen." The room went black and I felt faint. Akron shoved me, "They're calling you." I slowly stood and took the walk of shame through those doors. The nurse instructed me to remove my clothes from the waist down and to sit on the table and drape myself with a white cover. The doctor entered the room to start the procedure and I started sobbing. My legs were shaking so badly that the nurse had to give me a sedative. Finally, I calmed down enough to start the procedure. I watched the doctor grab a long silver instrument off the table, which he inserted into my womb to start the suction. The pain was like nothing I have ever felt. It felt as if my insides were being ripped out. After it was over, I promised myself that I would never put myself in that situation again, only to find myself pregnant again, six months later.

Our parents were furious! How could we be so careless as to let it happen again? This time was different. We were ready now, so we thought. In reality, we were no more ready that day than we were six months prior. We were just young kids being careless.

It is amazing how awesome God is. He will step in to save you from yourself.

Akron had just returned from his six weeks of basic training for the army. I was still in school and he was on his way to advanced military training. We had it all planned out. We were going to get married and become a happy family. Then one day, we were all at his mom's house enjoying the weekend as usual, and there was a knock at the door. The door was opened and there stood this light-skinned girl with long hair with a baby in her arms. Akron stood up, looked at me, I looked at him, and he looked at her. His face looked like he was seeing a ghost standing at the door. Everyone was confused as to who she was, but he walked over and invited her in, introducing her and the baby, as his son. I stood there in a state of shock. It felt like I had been hit by a Mack truck! I could not believe what I had just heard. His son! Everyone went goo-goo, gaga over the baby as I stood there, dazed and confused. How could he do this to me? How could everyone be so excited about the baby that just popped out of nowhere? They were supposed to be happy and excited about the baby I was carrying. My feelings were hurt and I hated everyone. To think, I was ready to give up my life to have a baby for him and this was how I was treated. He had betrayed me. He allowed that girl to come in and destroy our plans. What was the use of having this baby? At that moment, I decided I was not going through with this pregnancy! I told him and the family that since everyone was excited and overjoyed with little Joseph, I was not going to have our baby, but no one seemed to care at all.

As I laid in bed, curled up in a ball, holding my now lifeless stomach, I sulked in sorrow after the horrible experience I endured for the second time in less than eight months. Then I got a call from Akron's mom asking me to come over because they needed to talk to me. I arrived at their house, walked in, and he was sitting there looking crazy. I asked, "What is it?" He raised his hung head to say, "She was lying, little Joseph is not my baby. She said that because she wanted to get my military benefits. I am so sorry we turned our backs on you. Please forgive us." I sat there with mixed emotions – happy the baby was not his, but sad that I had killed my unborn child due to immaturity and insecurity.

Knowing that God was not pleased with my behavior and actions, I went to the altar to repent and ask for forgiveness. I also asked Him to give me the capacity to forgive those who I felt had wronged me. God did just that. Akron and I were able to mend our broken relationship. He gave me an engagement ring and we planned to be married after I graduated. Amidst our reconciliation and rekindling our relationship, I became pregnant again. I was 16, engaged, and my immature mind told me I was ready to take on the roles of mother and wife, not knowing how hard the journey was going to be. Akron was away finishing military training while I was home pregnant, working, and struggling to stay in school.

Finally, the day came to welcome our new baby boy into the world. It was the happiest day of our lives but also, the day our lives changed forever. It was hard to be a new mom and a senior in high school. The odds were stacked against me. Everyone said I would not finish school and that my life wouldn't amount to anything. However, I was determined not to be a statistic.

I did it! I graduated. I put on that gold cap and gown, held my head up high, walked across that stage, shook my principal's hand, and felt a great sense of accomplishment. I was a teen mom, but I did it.

Akron returned from training and tried to help and be support-ive, as best he could. However, things became overwhelming for both of us. We started arguing, fighting, and spending less qual-ity time together. Our relationship slid downhill. After much debate, I decided it was time to move on with my life. I called Akron and asked him if we could talk. After a long conversation and a lot of back and forth, I returned his engagement ring and told him our relationship was over. At this point, our only focus would be on our son.

At seventeen, I was a high school graduate and a single mom won-dering what I should do with my life. My primary objective was to be the best mother I could be and to raise my son in a happy, peaceful environment with an abundance of love. As I began to reevaluate my life, I was determined to make things better for Cornett and myself. I enrolled in school, found a full-time job, rededicated my life to Christ, and became active in my church again. Life was starting to look up.

Early one morning on a cold snowy winter day, I walked off the porch and started walking down the street with my book bags on my shoulder and my son planted on my hip. As I struggled with making my way to the bus stop, a car pulled up alongside me and a window was rolled down. Low and behold, it was Lorenzo. I could not believe my eyes. I hadn't seen him in almost three years. That all too familiar voice came from the driver's side saying, "It's too cold to be out here walking with a kid on your hip. Let me give you a ride." Without hesitation, I opened the back door, strapped my son under the seatbelt, threw in the book bags, and hopped in the front seat. I could not believe I was sitting in the car with Lorenzo, the man that I loved since I was 12 years old. This encounter took me back to the day he came to my house to get his drumsticks. I felt emotions that I didn't know I still had for him. I thought those emotions had been cast out into a sea of forgetfulness.

Day after day, he would come to pick us up, take me to work or school, and Cornett to daycare. It was as if we had become inseparable. I felt like I was at the beginning of my fairy tale. My knight in shining armor had returned. Little did I know that my fairy tale would soon turn into unbelievable episodes of Dr. Jekyll and Mr. Hyde. I had heard all about Lorenzo's criminal history and drug problem but I didn't care because that was his past. All I knew was that I loved him, and I felt I could love him enough to keep him on the straight and narrow, making him forget about that life.

Things were going great. Lorenzo showed me what real love was. His love surpassed every other love experience I ever had. He made me feel like I was the most important woman in the world. My mother didn't agree with us being together because of his age and his past. We would argue daily and she would forbid us from seeing each other. I was not having it. I was not going to let anything, or anyone come between us. "I am now 18 and pregnant with my second child. My son and I are moving out!" I yelled those words to my mom after the Cleveland Metro Housing Authority called to say, "You're approved for an apartment." We moved into the West 7th projects.

Finally, I was out on my own and able to be the queen of my castle. I thought to myself, this adult thing can't be that hard. I had convinced Lorenzo that living together would be the best thing for us. Everyone else thought it was a terrible idea but he moved in anyway. There were challenging days but overall things were good. He was working as a painter and playing the drums for the church on the weekend, and I was working at the plasma center. We were doing well for a young couple with two children. I was happy we were proving my friends and family wrong.

Then the day came when he introduced me to Mr. Hyde. We were sitting in the living room, watching television during our normal family time. Lorenzo rose from the couch, walked up the stairs, got his coat, and ran out the front door! I was confused as to what was going on. I jumped up, opened the door, and ran out to see where he had gone, and there was no sign of him. As I walked back into the apartment a little voice said to me, "Go check the drawer to see if the rent money is still there." I frantically ran up the stairs to find that my worse fear was confirmed. The drawer was open with clothes hanging out and the money sock was gone. The reality of what was happening hit me so hard, it knocked the wind out of me. I didn't know what to do. I couldn't call my family to tell them what happened as I didn't want to give them the satisfaction of being right. I sat down, trying to calm down and convince myself that I might be overreacting. As the evening progressed, I realized I was not overreacting. He was gone and he took every penny we had.

A few days passed and he had still not come back home. At this point, my sadness turned into anger. I grabbed the kids, put them in the car, and went out on a manhunt. We rode up and down the streets in the known drug area in the hood. Finally, we came upon a single cab pickup truck with three men sitting inside. I slowly approached and realized Lorenzo was the person in the middle. I stopped the car, jumped out, and starting yelling, "GET OUT THE CAR, GET OUT RIGHT NOW!" I was so overcome with anger that I forgot the kids were in the car. With hesitation, he emerged from the car, looking so bad, it brought tears to my eyes. His clothes were dirty, his lips were dry, cracked, and white and his eyes were bloodshot red. I could not believe my eyes. I didn't want the kids to see him like that, but I had to take him home. He stood there repeating, "I'm sorry," and brushed himself off as if that were going to change his appearance. I stood there wiping my tears away, trying to give the children the appearance that everything was ok. As we were riding home, I could hear my grandmother's voice saying, "What don't kill you only makes you stronger." That was the answer she gave to every tough situation we faced. That reminder was what I needed to hear to prepare me for what was to come.

As time went on the saga continued. We would have great moments, then terrible moments. However, I refused to give up. Through it all, we finally decided to get married after he was discharged from rehab. He promised that he was done with that life. He thanked me for my commitment and loyalty. As a young couple, him 25 and me 19, we were finally going to start living our fairy tale. We planned a beautiful wedding ourselves and a year later, the big day had finally arrived. Our day was magical. After everything was over, we packed the car with the gifts and a wishing well full of cards and money. We were both exhausted and decided to call it a night. We would pack for the honeymoon in the morning.

When the morning came, I woke up still feeling happy and excited, only to roll over to an empty bed. My first thought was, oh, he is packing the car and getting prepared for our trip. I walked downstairs to find all our wedding gifts and the wishing well gone! I opened the door to look out. The car was gone and he was nowhere in sight. I was devastated! I wanted to call the police, but I couldn't report that my husband had stolen our money and wedding gifts. Therefore, I had to remember, "What don't kill you only makes you stronger."

I went on to pretend that we had gone away on our honeymoon. I couldn't let anyone know what he had done. Day after day, I had to pretend that everything was going well. I couldn't stand the thought of the embarrassment if our families knew he had run out again. God was the only person I could turn to during my troubled time. Eventually, he came back home with his apology and a cry for help. I was his wife, I had to help him. Our marriage had become a cycle. Six months on, six months off. Things would be going great and then unexpectedly, he would disappear, taking every valuable thing we owned. This had become my life and I had become accustomed to it. However, I refused to be defeated. Determination was one of the key characteristics that my grandmother had instilled in me. I would wake up every morning praying, "Heavenly Father, I thank you for a new and refreshed day. I ask you for the will to push through, the strength to endure every obstacle I may be faced with today. Protect and keep my children as well as my husband. Change him Lord and renew his mind. In Jesus' holy name, I pray, Amen."

Prayer does change things, along with determination and perseverance. No matter how many obstacles you face, if you stay focused and don't give up, you can win. No one said it would be easy, but it is possible.

In July of 2002, I was able to walk across the stage to receive my BA in Criminal Justice and soon after was announced as the new

Admission Coordinator for the Ireland Cancer Center, earning over 50k a year at the age of 25. Lorenzo stopped using drugs and then started and grew his painting business, along with pursuing his music career. Life was good.

In 2012, Lorenzo was diagnosed with pancreatic cancer. At this point, we were divorced but remained the best of friends. The day before he took his last breath, my phone rang and on the other end, I heard a very weak voice that said, "Will you please forgive me? I know I took you through a lot. You never gave up on me. You showed me what unconditional love really means. You stayed strong for our three children and provide for our family when the streets had total control of me. For these things, I thank you, and I love you." I replied, "You're welcome. I forgive you and I will forever love you." I hung up the phone with a heavy heart, knowing the pain my children were about to endure.

My children took the death of their father very hard. However, it was my duty to remind them of the wonderful years they had with him and the love they shared. I encouraged my children to be strong and to always remember, "What don't kill you only makes you stronger."

ABOUT THE AUTHOR

Consuelo Allen is a proud mother of five and an even more overjoyed grandmother of two handsome grandsons and three beautiful granddaughters. She is a Certified Love Coach, Reiki Master, Author, Speaker, and Founder of Butterfly Beauti. Consuelo is passionate about helping others. Her loving and kind spirit makes it easy for her to be a servant leader. Consuelo is fiercely committed to serving others and acts as an advocate for children in foster care, troubled teens, and disabled individuals. Through a wealth of training, life experience, and knowledge, Consuelo had gained the skills and abilities to provide a plethora of services to her community. She believes is her duty to be a living example of dedication, hard work, and perseverance.

Over the years, it has been her mission to empower, encourage, and uplift others through acquiring tools and techniques that have proven to help individuals find their true selves. Through many trials and tribulations, she has found the strength to push forward and continue to help others, displaying the true meaning of selflessness.

Follow her on Facebook at
www.Facebook/Butterflybeauti.com
or coachconnie@consueloallen.com

CHAPTER 7

Broken Dreams

by Kenyatta Collins

As a child, I remember the enjoyment I had whenever I played with my dolls. I would religiously change their clothes: pajamas for bed, dresses for Sundays, play clothes for outside. I made my dolls do the same thing my parents made me do. It seemed logical to me. I would even fix their hair into what I considered to be the most elaborate styles my little hands could manage, often using the same bows and ribbons that my mother would use to do my hair. Whenever it came time for us, as a family, to leave home for the day, I made sure to bring at least one of my dolls along for the ride. From Cabbage Patch Kids to My Kid Sister, Rainbow Brite, and even Baby Alive, you name it, I had it. For me, they were more than just dolls, they were my babies.

I was the oldest of my parents' two children, so I did my share of helping with my little brother. I can recall an incident when he was crying and I took it upon my four-year-old self to go check-in on him. Next thing you know, my mother hears this loud thump from the living room and runs frantically to her bedroom. She thought my brother had fallen off the bed when it was me creating all the ruckus. I had picked up my little brother and held him tightly as I hopped off the bed with him in my arms. We were both safe, to my mother's relief. The nurturing instinct has always been in me. I still had my dolls but now I had a real baby to care for too. As many young girls do, I dreamt of someday having a perfect life and a perfect family of my own, and it all seemed so simple when I was little. Unfortunately, we don't always get what we want as the road we call life is forever twisting and turning.

For the most part, while I was growing up, things went pretty much as planned. I graduated high school with a full-ride scholarship to college. High school and college came and went with their own set of events but life was good. I ended up working in banking for a while after graduation as my initial interest in law school had changed. I knew I wanted to be in a field to help others, but I figured out early on it wasn't going to be through law.

On May 2, 2008, I gave birth to my daughter, Liberty. When they positioned her little body on my chest that day in the delivery room, I couldn't do anything but cry tears of joy.

As my mother wiped my tears away, I could see that she too had tears cascading down her cheeks. Ten fingers, ten toes… my baby girl was perfect in every sense, and I was over the moon in love with her. When she was only six months old, her father and I went our separate ways and for many reasons, I feel this was for the best. Never in a million years did I ever envision myself being a single mother, but I took the challenge and I learned so much about myself during that time. I was stronger than I ever gave myself credit for. That same strength, unknown to me, would someday be tested again.

Later that year through mutual friends I reconnected with Chuck, a long-time close friend who I had dated in the past. I sent him a simple "guess who" text message and the rest was history. Three-hour telephone conversations turned into dates and the dates blossomed into a full-on relationship. From the beginning, he was very empathetic of my circumstances and made it clear that he knew dating me meant accepting my child as well. He treated her as his own from the very beginning.

By the summer of 2011, we were engaged, and I was moving to Atlanta, Georgia with my daughter to prepare for a future with the love of my life. I enrolled in nursing school the following year to complete classes I had begun while living in Louisville, Kentucky. After interacting with the nurses in the hospital during my daughter's birth, when I had mild complications from pre-eclampsia, I decided that nursing was where I not only wanted to be but needed to be. The same compassion, service, and patience they exuded towards me were exactly what I wanted to share with others. This was embedded in me from birth. Service was my gift, and I was committed to finishing school.

After months of planning the perfect wedding, while also attending nursing school, Chuck and I tied the knot in the summer of 2013. I couldn't believe it… I had married my best friend and soul mate. Our new life together was just beginning and like any newlywed couple, we had so many plans for our lives. Places to, things to do, and a lifetime of memories to create. Life was looking up and we were ready to take it all in.

By the winter of the next year, I was walking across the stage accepting my bachelor's degree. I did it! I had finished nursing school. Because I was already working at Grady (one of Atlanta's most reputable trauma hospitals) as a nurse intern, I was fortunate enough to continue working there after graduating. Our plans were unfolding right before us and we couldn't be more grateful. It wasn't long after this that we began to entertain the possibility of expanding our little family.

Because I was into my thirties and years had passed since my first child, I wanted to make sure everything was ok before we began trying to conceive. I made appointments with just about everybody. I went to my OB/GYN, my primary doctor, and yes, even a cardiologist. I was given the green light by my healthcare team that July and we got right to it. We tracked my ovulation schedule and planned which months I could conceive so we didn't waste any time. I was thrilled about having a child with my husband and wanted to bear his firstborn.

By September of the same year, we were pregnant. After investing a small fortune on a home pregnancy test, I already knew I was pregnant but needed confirmation, so I immediately scheduled an appointment with my OB/GYN. After having a quick ultrasound and bloodwork, I was taken to an exam room. There, I would try to make out my ultrasound images, read and re-read all the pamphlets on the wall, and start to let my mind wander about the joys of pregnancy as I waited impatiently for my doctor to arrive. "Congratulations!" my doctor exclaimed, as he walked in handing me a sheet of paper about pregnancy. It turns out that I was only about four and a half weeks pregnant so I would need to return in a few weeks for another visit. The muscles in my face tightened as a delighted smile crept across it.

I don't believe I even made it to the car before I told my husband and soon after my mom. The good news traveled fast and before I made it home, I had multiple congratulatory texts and calls. It seemed like an eternity as I awaited my husband's arrival home from work that day. I greeted him at the front door with the ultrasound photos. We stood there focusing on the small greyish-black dot on the images that would someday be our little one.

Weeks later we returned to the OB/GYN for my follow-up appointment. This was the day we were going to listen to our baby's heartbeat for the very first time. We were beyond thrilled. "Alright, you guys ready?" the tech questioned as she gathered the equipment and turned on the monitor. We could see an image on the screen but where was the swoosh, swoosh, swoosh, swooshing of our baby's heart we longed to hear? Moments passed but still, no heartbeat. I could tell that the tech felt something was wrong as she continued to maneuver the wand around inside of me looking for various angles and graphing measurements on the screen. As I lay on the table, I looked over to Chuck and without words, I knew we were thinking the same thing. "Why don't I hear my baby's heartbeat?" I muffled, holding back tears. "Are you sure about how many weeks you are?" the tech cautiously replied. "Yes," my voice quivered.

Back in the exam room, our fears were confirmed, I was having a miscarriage. Our baby had stopped growing around week six and we were faced with deciding if we would wait it out at home and let nature take its course or head to the hospital. I couldn't handle that. We couldn't handle that. I opted to have a procedure called a D&C and was scheduled to report to the hospital. After everything was said and done, we were left to our understanding of things. Many couples experience miscarriages, so maybe it was for the better and the next time things would be different. Right?

Slowly, we managed to get back to life as we knew it. I continued to work diligently in my field and decided to take things to the next level and applied to a Master of Nursing program. I was accepted and scheduled to begin in the fall of 2016. To our surprise, we learned that we were pregnant in April of that year. I remember being so excited and wanting to tell everyone, yet at the same time no one at all. Only our parents would know this time, at least until I was further along.

The pregnancy was going well, and weight was lifted off our shoulders after I made it past the twelve-week mark. Whew! Now we could finally tell more of our friends and family. That summer we even traveled to New York with my parents and had the most amazing trip ever. In the airport, my parents went their way to head back to Kentucky and we went ours to head back to Atlanta. Wait a minute… what was this? I felt the moisture between my legs, almost as if I had peed a little but I hadn't. I made my way to the bathroom as I normally would before boarding, trying not to alarm my husband or my daughter. "Lord, please don't let me be bleeding," I thought on my way to the stall.
It turned out that I wasn't bleeding at all but why did I have this leaking suddenly? I told my husband about this event and that I planned to check in with my doctor when we got home.

Leaving the airport, we headed to a friend's house to pick up our dog as she had been watching it for us and again, I went to the bathroom. This time, when I sat down to pee it felt like a water balloon had just burst. The water gushed out with such force that it reached the wall in front of me. "Chuuuuuuck!" I screeched out in a tone that invoked chills. Fear crept in as I began to think the worst. We proceeded to go to the Emergency Room where it was discovered that my water had indeed ruptured while my cervix remained closed. There was still some fluid present but the baby was ok.

I was prescribed antibiotics to decrease the risk of infection to me and my unborn baby until I could come into the office. We were given the ok by my obstetrician to go to Kentucky for a couple of days to see my husband's mother who had just been diagnosed with multiple myeloma cancer which prevented her from traveling with us to New York. I had orders to maintain strict bed rest with bathroom privileges only for the duration of our stay. I'll admit, it was comforting to be amongst the family during such uncertainty, but I just couldn't help but think about what news we would be facing when we returned home.

Upon returning home, I went to see a fetal-maternal specialist and had yet another ultrasound completed. We were taken down a long hall to the doctor's personal office. This had never happened before. My stomach tightened. The doctor walked in, took a seat, and looked me dead in my eyes as she told me what little fluid I had before was now completely gone. She stated that my baby would no longer have any room to grow and, under these conditions, could not live.

The words were like swords cutting to my core. The lump in my throat tightened as the tears formed and rolled down my face. My husband held me tight in his arms. Was there nothing I could do? Could we replace the fluid? Did I do something wrong? As a nurse, I knew the answers, but as a mother willing to do anything to protect her unborn child, I asked anyway. With P.R.O.M. (premature rupture of membranes) there was no fixing it, it is just "something that happens," and in my case, it happened for no foreseen reason.

Leaving the office, we exited from a side door to avoid having to go back through the waiting room with all the other expectant mothers. Because my baby still had a heartbeat, I hung on to the possibility that maybe a miracle would happen. I couldn't bring myself to even fathom making any drastic decisions and opted to wait. A few days later at the office of the OB/GYN, in the same room, I received news of my first miscarriage, I was told that my baby had passed, and I would need to go to the hospital to be induced. That night at home we broke the news to my then 8-year-old daughter, and as a parent, this was one of the hardest things to do. She had been so excited about becoming a big sister and just couldn't understand why God had taken her sibling away. She ran off to her room and returned with a note asking God to watch over her little brother or sister and that she was thankful she had an angel in heaven. My heart was like a sinking ship.

The next morning, I was checked into the hospital for a scheduled induction. On August 3, 2016, I gave birth to our son, Princeton Ali Collins, at only seventeen and a half weeks pregnant. His frail little body laid curled in the palm of my hand as if he were still in my womb. "Mommy loves you," I whispered as I kissed his cold tiny head. My husband and I shared a brief moment with Princeton before the nurse carried him away. I fell back onto my tear-stained pillow, staring blankly at the ceiling while clenching my husband's hand.

Nothing in life could have ever prepared me for that moment. Coming to the delivery suite was supposed to be a joyous occasion, however, for us, it was a nightmare. We left the hospital empty and broken carrying only a box filled with items for moms who had lost their babies. Days later we went to Donehoo-Lewis, a local funeral home that offered cremation services for premature babies. There, I was given the emotional task of selecting an urn for our son's remains. *Please, somebody, pinch me… hurry.* This was entirely too much.

Ironically, I was slated to begin my Master of Nursing program in just a few short days. How was I going to do it? Could I do it? I couldn't even go a day without weeping. How was I going to handle having to focus on helping others when I didn't even have answers to help myself? By the grace of God, I was able to muster up enough strength to make it through the class orientation. I smiled and even carried on conversations with others. This was easier than expressing my true feelings. It's funny how no one ever questions a smile.

Back at home, my life was like a rollercoaster ride. I would be fine one moment, and the next I was researching possible causes as to why this could have happened to me. I questioned everything and everyone, including God. All I wanted was to have a child with my husband. Was this too much to ask?

Intimacy after the loss of our son was hyperemotional and had to be approached like a delicate flower. Often, being held was as much as I could mentally tolerate before sobbing uncontrollably.

I wanted to be intimate with my husband more than anything but another part of me wanted to curl into a ball. Weeks passed before I was able to fully succumb to having sex. Ultimately, my tears dwindled and our sex life began shifting in the right direction. Maybe time can heal all wounds.

In going through this turmoil, we discovered that a couple of close friends had also gone through traumatic experiences during past pregnancies. Although their stories were different from ours, we still found comfort in knowing that we at least had someone that could relate to us. Between the demands of school and a host of family and friends surrounding us with love and compassion, I regained a little more of myself each day. I began to look through the glass and see it as half full versus half empty. I still had my daughter, my life, and my marriage. At this moment, I knew I couldn't allow what had happened to me, to us, to get the best of me. There was more to my story and I decided to keep moving forward.

Days turned into weeks and weeks into months as I ground my way through the first year of my master's program. Working while I was in school was hectic, but I held onto the fact that nothing worth having would come easy. The chaos of it all may have even been therapeutic for me in some sense. I challenged myself to be the best at what I did, not for anyone else's gratitude but simply for myself. At least with this, unlike my pregnancies, I could have some part in how things turned out.

In the summer of 2017 after an amazing trip to Puerto Rico, I found out that I was pregnant once again. This wasn't anything intentional but at the same time, there was nothing in place to prevent it from happening either. I didn't share this news with a soul initially, besides my husband. With all that had already transpired, they wouldn't understand the desire I had to have a child with my husband, or would they? Because I wanted a different perspective this time around, I opted to find a new OB/GYN office. After interviewing a host of locations, I settled on one in Fayetteville, Georgia that checked all the boxes for prenatal care and high-risk pregnancies. After all, I was high-risk.

After my first visit to the new doctor's office, I received a call a day or so later about something of concern in my labs and I needed to come in right away. Panic overcame me and breath left my body as I slumped over a nearby counter in disbelief. A co-worker insisted on driving me to the doctor's office as I was in no shape to do so. The ride there remains a blur as I only recall walking through the sliding doors and taking the elevator to the third floor. Moments later my husband and daughter joined me. What were they about to tell me? I thought to myself.

After what seemed like an eternity, the back-office door opened. "Mrs. Collins?" a nurse questioned, looking for a taker. I stood, with weak knees and a knot in my stomach, and followed her to the back. I went to Ultrasound and then to one of those cold exam rooms. "Lord, please give me strength," I prayed silently. The doctor walked in and proceeded to tell me that based on my pregnancy levels and the ultrasound, I was having an ectopic pregnancy that could eventually rupture. I might as well have been punched in the gut from the way her words resonated in me. Not again!!!

My pregnancy was over before it even began. For several weeks I returned to the office for bloodwork to ensure that my hormone levels came back down safely. Sitting in the waiting room was probably the hardest thing. There I would be, amidst a crowd of glowing moms-to-be, waiting to have labs drawn that would further confirm that that wasn't going to be me, yet again. What did I do to deserve this? Was I being punished? Questions flooded my mind.

Months later, I found myself back at my original OB/GYN office seeking answers as to why this continued to happen to me. We knew there wasn't an issue with me getting pregnant: my cervix was fine, my uterus was healthy, and I had carried a baby to term in the past. There was no scientific reason(s) identified that could explain why. I investigated sunup and sundown studying statistics, risks, and causes of what I had experienced over the past three years when all I wanted was a glimmer of hope...hope that I still had a chance of giving my husband a child of his own.

With a seed of hope and a renewed spirit, my husband and I agreed to try one...more... time. The fourth time is a charm, right?! As before, I became pregnant within a couple of months of trying. I knew this was a blessing in and of itself as many women struggle with becoming pregnant. I was grateful for every milestone.

With this pregnancy, I pushed fear to the side early on, refusing to let my mind wander down the rabbit hole. I went to every doctor's appointment expecting nothing less than good news as I knew every pregnancy was different. Because I was now thirty-five years old, which is considered an advanced maternal age, I had to endure a few extra genetic tests, but prayerfully, everything came back normal. Due to past complications, my OB/GYN discussed having me start Makena progesterone injections to help decrease the risk of another spontaneous birth along with a more frequent visit with the fetal-maternal specialist over the coming weeks.

We elected to share the news of our upcoming rainbow baby with all our friends and family. In January 2018, at sixteen and a half weeks pregnant, we went in for my ultrasound that would determine the sex of our baby. We did not care whether it was a boy or girl, we just wanted a healthy baby. When we heard our baby's strong heart beating on the monitor, that was more than enough for us. Another milestone, thank you, Jesus.

We took our sealed envelope containing the sex of the baby back home to Kentucky that weekend for a gender reveal I had been strategically planning. It was such a beautiful occasion. As we cut into the cake, we were all elated to learn we were having a GIRL! I already knew what her name would be and instantly began decorating her room in my mind.

We returned home in time for me to receive my first Makena injection a few days later. If this were the one thing that I could do to protect my unborn child, I was willing to endure it for however long. I only had one year left of my graduate program and I was excited about how our lives were shaping up. I was still working full-time, twelve-hour shifts at Grady, but I knew that within a few months I would probably need to cut my hours back to alleviate any undue stress during the pregnancy, a decision that brought relief to many.

A week later, the doorbell rang bright and early, as the home nurse had arrived to administer my second injection. Nothing formal she checked my vitals, gathered the supplies, and before you knew it, she was out the door leaving me with a sore butt cheek and a Band-Aid. Upstairs, I began to get myself ready for the appointment that I had later that day with the fetal-maternal specialist. I chatted with my husband through the bathroom door as I sat down to pee. Within seconds, water gushed out everywhere! My heart raced in disbelief as my mind flashed images of the past. My husband felt my energy by the way I shrieked for him. This was more than déjà vu.

Needless to say, we got to our appointment a lot sooner than we had initially planned that day. After having an ultrasound, we were escorted back down the same dreadful hallway to meet with the same doctor that told me about Princeton just two years prior. Without rhyme or reason history was repeating itself. My joy was stripped from me with just a few simple words… "Your membranes have ruptured, and the baby has no fluid." My blood boiled, my eyes teared up, and I could barely breathe. It took everything in me not to scream and yell at the top of my lungs. I hated this situation!! I prayed like a crazy woman that my baby could make it just a couple more weeks so that she could maybe, just maybe, have a chance at survival. Instead, a couple of days later when I was admitted to the hospital, her little heart had already stopped beating. At eighteen and a half weeks pregnant I gave birth to my little princess, Parker Danielle Collins, on January 26, 2018. We cherished her presence quietly as a family, each of us holding her for a brief moment and saying our good-byes. I could see the love my daughter had for her sister as she held and admired her tiny body. My heart broke all over again.

There are moments where no matter what words are said, they never reach your soul. This was one of those times. I was surrounded by family and friends during this time yet felt completely hollow on the inside. As a parent, having to go back to the same funeral home for the cremation of another one of your children was simply unfair. Sitting in the parking lot of the funeral home, I was paralyzed by the thought of having to select an urn for my baby instead of clothes or nursery décor. The funeral home director simply embraced me once I was inside as he too was at a loss for words.

Conversations at home were uncomfortable as no one knew how best to console the other or what their temperament would be. I had lost another child, he had lost another opportunity to have a biological child, and my daughter had lost another sibling. It was like walking on eggshells. At one point, I agreed to be placed on medication for depression for a short period, just to help me cope, something I had initially refused. Hearing my daughter in the distance asking my husband if mommy was going to be okay was enough for me.

My husband and I eventually attended a counseling session to help us to at least acknowledge what we each needed to heal. It was during this pivotal time that I saw just how strong my marriage was. I was truly blessed. Yes, I wanted to have a child with and for my husband, but it was deeper than that. The commitment between us never once faltered…it became stronger.

In time, I began to accept that it was okay to not be okay. I allowed myself to embrace and own every aspect of the grieving process. This was my story. One thing I learned is that when you persevere through what I would consider hell, you develop a new outlook on life. I chose to live my life fully. The things that used to consume my time, with angst, didn't seem so concerning anymore. Fears I once entertained were now small and insignificant. I loved my family harder than ever and took nothing for granted.

I stopped wallowing in my sorrow and used that energy to change my narrative. I will agree, some days were harder than others to peel myself out of bed, so I made sure to encircle myself with positivity every chance I could. Daily devotionals, positive affirmations, and optimistic individuals were my ammo. Through one of the most trying times in my life, I was able to help my husband birth businesses. I pushed myself to finish my graduate program so that I may continue to operate in my God-given gift. I became a life coach so that I could share my story to help others see their true potential, not just their past. I became a global missionary to show God's love while providing aid to those in need.

Today, I often find myself smiling as I pull up to my home because I appreciate God's favor over my life. The perfect life and family that I dreamt of as a child greets me every time I walk through the doors, and I am grateful for that. Yes, I miss my angel babies very much and think of them daily, but I have peace knowing they continue to watch over us. Life doesn't always go as planned, that is for sure, but we must know that our mountains don't define us, they simply add character.

ABOUT THE AUTHOR

KENYATTA COLLINS, MSN, APRN, FNP-C, CLC

Kenyatta N. Collins was born on November 16, 1982, in Louisville, KY. She attended the University of Louisville graduating with a Bachelor of Arts degree in Political Science in 2005. She made the move to the state of Georgia in 2011 where she now resides with her husband (Chuck) and daughter (Liberty) in McDonough, GA. She received her Bachelor of Science and Master of Science in Nursing from Clayton State University in 2014 and 2019 respectively. Kenyatta currently works as a reputable nurse practitioner in McDonough, with goals to eventually run her own practice. She also dreams of starting up health clinics abroad for poverty-stricken nations.

Kenyatta and her family attend Tabernacle of Praise Church International where she is an avid member of the global mission's team with recent travels to South Africa and Jamaica. Since becoming a certified Life Coach, Kenyatta has launched BLOOM by Kenyatta where she strives to promote health, women's empowerment, self-love, and healing. Kenyatta is also the co-founder/

CEO of 22 Enterprises LLC, a local Atlanta business that special-izes in trucking, real estate, and other investments. She serves on the Board for Coaching Forward International Inc., and The Frances Harbin Brown Foundation Inc. Upcoming projects include podcasts, speaking engagements, and book signings.

For booking information please visit
www.kenyattacollins.com
or www.BLOOMbyKenyatta.com
for more information.

CHAPTER 8

The Strength is in the Struggle

by Mia Colemon

Struggle is Real

"But his answer was: My grace is all you need, for my power is greatest when you are weak. I am most happy, then, to be proud of my weaknesses, in order to feel the protection of Christ's power over me. I am content with weaknesses, insults, hardships, persecutions, and difficulties for Christ's sake. For when I am weak, then I am strong." 2 Corinthians 12:9-10

What does struggle look like to you? Broken relationships, failed marriages, grief, a stale career, depression, anxiety, fear, and feelings of inadequacy? A struggle can look and feel different but your attitude and mindset during your struggle can be the catalyst that projects you into the next level of your situation. Something that may be very minuscule to you can be a catastrophic mess to someone else. Although the word struggle can have many different definitions, one thing I think we can agree on is that the struggle, whatever it may be, is very real. I remember going through a few different life challenges over the last 15 years that I thought would surely make me lose my mind. Yet no matter what my struggle in life was, I always heard the voice of the Lord saying to me, "Your strength is in your struggle." I kept asking myself how in the world could there be any strength in my struggle? Especially when I felt alone, I felt like God was nowhere near me, I felt trapped in a box and yet sometimes I felt like I was so exposed that the world could see every intricate detail of my life. I questioned God, I questioned myself. Thoughts ran through my mind like, "You are a bad mom," "You will never get through this," "You are not a good wife," and "You are a failure." Yes…I was a Christian woman, raised in the church, and still, I could remember very succinctly that I felt lonely. No, I was lonely. I could not see that I could make it no matter what the situation was. I could not see that God was right there with me and he had never left me. I could not see that my struggles did not determine the strength that I had within myself. I could not let go of those six words – your strength is in your struggle. I knew that I was not alone and that others needed to hear the same encouraging words that I had heard and managed to live by daily. No matter what the situation looked like to me and those around me, I knew that I could overcome and find strength during these struggles.

I invite you to come along with me on this journey to finding your strength in the struggle. I pray that the words on these pages resonate with you and produce actions and accountability in your life. I pray that you can find the courage to conquer your struggles, encouragement, empowerment, and more importantly your voice during the storms of life. Your voice of reason, hope, wisdom, and the strength to overcome whatever struggles you may face in life.

"Each one, as a good manager of God's different gifts, must use for the good of others the special gift he has received from God." I Peter 4:10 GNT

The plan for my life was in place before I was conceived in my mother's womb. I was born to a single mom just shy of her twentieth birthday and soon to become the oldest of six siblings. First to arrive, first in charge; a natural-born leader. Did you hear me? Firstborn, a natural leader and little did I know, a life that was destined to bless others. My life was not free of roadblocks and setbacks, I would have my fair share of trials and tribulations but through it all, I learned to trust in God and overcome every snare and trap that the enemy set in my path. Let us take a journey and see how I overcame them.

The Struggle of an Absent Father

I was born on April 9, 1968. My mother was from a little town in Western Pennsylvania where everyone knew everyone, and it was not uncommon for a person to be related to each other more than once on the family tree. I'm sure you understand what I mean by this statement. My father came from a semi-well put together family in a suburban town outside of Cincinnati, Ohio, not necessarily rich but his mother cleaned a home for a wealthy Caucasian family in Glendale, Ohio. It would be easy for an outsider to consider them as a well-off middle-class family. Like most African American families, both my family and my father's family were as normal as a family could be in the late '60s and early '70s, you know the adage "what goes on in this house stays in this house?" Neither families were free from life's spots nor wrinkles but I still grew up being proud of my background. My mother often told me the story of how when my father found out she was pregnant with me, he denied me from the start. He even went as far as to tell his mother that I was not his baby. It wasn't until years later that my nana would tell my mom that when she came to visit me as a newborn in the hospital, that she went back and told my dad, "John Richard, either you're lying or that's Ace's baby." Ace Freeman was my grandfather and apparently, I graced this world looking just like Paw Paw Ace. So, there I was a light-skinned, big-eyed baby girl born to a single mom that lived with her aunt because she was trying to have a better life than she had with her parents. Her life at home with her mother and father was tumultuous, to say the least. Sure, most of the time she grew up in a two-parent household but not without experiencing alcohol, abuse, and heartaches. One thing I know for sure and that is my mom used her life as an example and the core values that she instilled in me would prove to be lifelong lessons that I would utilize well into my adult life.

Growing up, my father was not present in my life most of the time. There was always an excuse as to why he was not accepting his responsibilities. My mom received $25 child support payments because my father worked sparingly. Mom never spoke badly of my natural father and she always reminded me that he was my father and I had to respect him. She allowed me to visit my grandmother as much as her finances would permit; sometimes my father was present and sometimes he was not. I was a teenager when his wife told me that he had gone through their entire savings account in a short period. It was then that I would come to know that my father was not only an absentee father but also a drug addict. In my world, he was absent in the physical and mental sense, but I still knew in my heart that I was not fatherless. My mother made sure that although I did not have the presence of my natural father in my life, I was never without the Father, God. I knew at a young age that the Lord destined my plan for life to reach out to others, give to others, and encourage others. I knew that I was not on this journey of life by myself, I was designed to reach out and touch everyone in a special way. I never want to leave people the same after my encounter with them, I want to plant a seed of love, hope, and encouragement into their lives. Although I was denied a relationship with my natural father, I knew too well that I was never without my spiritual father in heaven.

Struggling to be Saved yet Feeling Bound

Religion was very important in our home. I accepted Jesus Christ at the age of nine, but it was not of my own free will. I would go to church every week, often several times a week, and fall asleep in service. I remember one Sunday afternoon on the car ride home from church, my mom asked me when I was going to stop sleeping in church. To my surprise, I responded that I didn't know, to which my mom replied, "Today was your last day." The next major milestone in my spiritual journey was water baptism. Do you remember when you were sanctified, you tarried for the Holy Ghost? This logic was never clear in my mind, but I do not know how it would be clear in the mind of a nine-year-old young lady. Nevertheless, I tarried until I received the Holy Ghost with the evidence of speaking in tongues. We were a part of a very authoritarian religious organization. We could not wear pants or shorts and I never experienced attending dances or even participating in my high school prom. I was teased and ridiculed as early as in elementary school because I was considered "a saved nerd." As I entered my teenage years and high school, regrets filled my heart because I knew that I was missing out on very important milestones that my friends could participate in. Although I was technically saved at a young age, I would not really come to know Jesus until later in my adult life. My mother always taught me that just because we were not permitted to go to or do certain things, it didn't mean that I wasn't saved or that I'd go to hell like we were often taught at church. She explained that we did things a certain way because we were obedient to the rules of the church. Now, I know you are probably wondering how in the world could a person be raised in the church and not like it? This is my truth – I wanted to be able to do what all my friends were doing. I somehow thought that If I could be like my friends, I would not be shunned. I remember going off to college and I began to experience things that I couldn't participate in at home, like partying, my first official boyfriend, and friends who did things very differently than from the way I was raised.

My pastor worked as a custodian at the college that I attended. I remember wanting to try out for the band but he told me absolutely, no. I was disobedient and did it anyway, so the pastor sat me down. Being sat down was a church tradition that in my mind served as punishment where one was not permitted to work in the church for an extended period. When young ladies would become pregnant out of wedlock, they were put in front of the entire church to confess and ask for forgiveness. I thought that this process or punishment, as I referred to it in my mind, was a process to ridicule and embarrass an individual and it was my breaking point for dealing with the church. I realized that I didn't want to be a part of a community, organization, or structure that operated in bondage and fear.

At that time, I didn't know that Jesus gave us all free will but I would later learn this when I accepted Christ as my personal Lord and savior for the second time, only this time, I had a complete understanding of what being a Christian meant. So, there I was, year two of college, miserably failing most of my classes. I knew that I was on a short rope to being academically kicked out of college, but remember the plan that I said God had for me? It was all in his plan. I knew that I couldn't return home because that would mean attending a church that I despised. I know that despise is a strong word, but truth be told, it was how I felt deep within. I wanted no connection with what I knew to be called "the church" and its rules. My self-esteem was at an all-time low. I felt like a failure; like I didn't have a purpose for my life. But I knew that for the last two years I was basically on my own and I knew that I had to grow up quickly because I could not go back home.

I joined the Marine Corps because I was running from home and church, and my heart had been broken by my first boyfriend. I didn't feel that I had any purpose, and my self-esteem was at an all-time low. I completed 13 weeks of boot camp and ended up being stationed in Okinawa, Japan. I was just shy of my 21st birthday and over 7,000 miles from what I knew to be home. Joining the Marine Corps was one of the best decisions that I had made so far in my life. The process helped me to mature, become a confident young lady, walk with my head up, and changed my mindset about how I felt about myself and my life. From Parris Island to Okinawa, Japan, to Camp Lejeune, I would meet and develop lifelong friendships. Sisters and friends that were not afraid to hold me accountable or rejoice in my wins, were always there for me to uplift and encourage me. This was truly a network of friends that I knew as family.

The Struggle of Comparison

Have you ever had that one friend that no matter how they acted in life they always seemed to have nice things? Win at everything? Always be on top of the world? You know, the fancy car, big house on the lake, perfect husband, awesome career. I mean, what more could they ask for, right? When you look at their life and compare it to yours, you are overcome with feelings of jealousy, bitterness, and inadequacy. The reason we struggle with insecurity is that we see other's situations from the outside and we compare what we see to what we have. So, you see, the struggle of insecurity goes hand in hand with the struggle of comparison. Take social media for example. We are living in an age where Facebook, Snapchat, Twitter, and Instagram can impact our lives. We see others posting what they want us to think their life looks like. More times than not it is just one big façade. We don't know that they only have one hundred dollars in their bank account the day after payday, that they are about to be evicted from the house that they rent, and that the car they drive is a lease. They only show the world the glamorous parts of life or so it seems. They could have it all together and still be depressed, lonely, unhappy, and one step from throwing in the towel. You see, your struggle in comparing yourself to others is because you are on the outside looking through the window and you have no idea what is going on behind closed doors. It is all designed to make you see something that looks attractive and desirable. Not knowing that what you see with the naked eye is a disastrous situation for most. We all have different paths to walk in this life and not one person's journey is the same. Comparing yourself to others opens the door for their actions to begin to control your actions. You waste so much energy when you focus your attention on what other people are doing, accomplishing, and achieving in their lives.

In Galatians 6:4-5 in the Amplified Bible, Classic Edition, it says, *"But let every person carefully scrutinize and examine and test his own conduct and his own work. He can then have the personal satisfaction and joy of doing something commendable [alone] without [resorting to] boastful comparison with his neighbor."* When we can discover that we know who our provider, protector, friend, and savior is, we do not have to worry about comparing our life to anyone. Psalm 23:1 Good News Translation says, *"The Lord is my shepherd; I have everything I need."* If you have everything that you need, then you do not have to compare yourself to anyone or anything. Do not waste another minute of your time chasing someone else's dream, as what is for you is for you and no one else. Focus on your dreams and what it is you want to accomplish.

Practice the art of journaling and at the beginning of every month set small attainable goals. Create a small vision board to remind you of things that you would like to accomplish throughout the year. On your vision board paste pictures of a place where you would like to take a vacation, a piece of jewelry that you have been eyeing, a weight loss goal, and the list could go on and on. You must wake up every day with a mindset to choose happiness and abundance. Freely take God's grace and mercy as a gift; this journey is yours to own. Be fully committed to becoming all that God has designed for you to be.

The Struggle to Trust

"Trust in the Lord with all of your heart and lean not on your own understanding; in all your ways submit to him, and he will make your paths straight." Proverbs 3:5-6 (NIV).

The moment we can get out of our head and release control… that is the moment God can begin to work, and things will begin to change for us.

One morning, I woke up early and stumbled my way to the bathroom. As I was walking in the dark, I noticed that after a few seconds my eyes adjusted to the darkness, and even though there were no lights on to guide me, I could still see well enough to get to my destination. After I laid back down in bed, I started to pray and I thought about how I never reached for the light switch, but my eyes adjusted on their own. I thought to myself, Mia, that's exactly how God wants you to trust him, in your moments of uncertainty, when the path is not always clear. He wants us to trust him enough to know that he will refocus our sight and make things clear so that we can see our way through the storms of life. However, we often reach for the lights and do not give God time to do what He needs to do for us. Do not let your current situations or moments of darkness cause you to lose focus on Him.

When I decided to join the Marine Corps, if someone would have told me that one day I would be placed in front of women to speak a word of hope and encouragement to them, I would have said, "The devil is a lie." Remember, I was the church nerd, was bullied, had no self-esteem, suffered from a fatherless life, and my heart had been broken a time or two. I had no intention of ever being the person that would lend a listening ear to anyone. After all, my small problems were enough to keep me in my co-coon for life…so I thought. But I realized that at every step of my journey, I had one gift that kept coming to the surface and was beginning to come to fruition in my life and that was the gift of service to others. I could listen without judgment, hear others with a spirit of empathy, and give feedback and constructive criticism in love. I always found myself telling my friends and family, "I am here for you." I always knew that if anything in life was easy, it really would not be worth doing. When God gives you the vision, he will bless you with the tools necessary to carry out your dreams and plans.

Every year in December, I always take time to reflect on the months behind me and I write down goals of what I want to accomplish in the upcoming new year. In December 2017, during my reflection time, I knew that all the signs were there for me to become a Certified Life Coach. I completed my Life Coach certification in November 2018 and birthed my dream, Be Intentional 4 Life, Life Coaching. My platform is a place where the hearts and minds of women come to be encouraged, inspired, and uplifted.

Often, we as women are experiencing the same hardships and trials in life, but we are fearful of what others may say, or how they will perceive us, and many times are just downright ashamed of what we have overcome, so we don't share our testimony. We think, Lord how I did I get here or what was I thinking? We put up with physical and mental abuse all in the name of what we think is LOVE. We turn to things like drugs, alcohol, people, and situations that we know are not good for our well-being. Here is where we get caught up, and we substitute people, places, and things instead of turning to our Father to be all that we need Him to be for us. I never knew how God would use me until I stepped out of my comfort zone in faith and learned to trust him completely. Building trust completely in the Lord is a hard test to pass and most of us fail this test more times than not. We let our emotions, feelings, and strong will get in the way. We know that God has never failed us yet, but sometimes we want to pray, turn it over to God and then try to navigate how He does things for us. We bargain with God; we try to rush Him and sometimes we quit and try to do it ourselves. To have faith in God we must learn to control our emotions, speak positive affirmations continually, and fully drown ourselves in His word. You must get up every day and make the decision that you are going to trust in the Lord and not lean towards your own understanding. Walking in faith and trusting the Lord is a decision that you must turn into action every day. We can either choose to worship the Lord or worry about things in our life that we said we would trust Him to take care of for us. No matter what we have gone through in life, only He can make the painful parts of our lives beautiful. I could have let my emotions and thoughts deter me from my calling because the voice in my head said, "Girl, you know you aren't qualified to help anyone, no one wants to hear what you have to say, and they aren't interested in your story." But listen, if God already knows all before we were ever conceived in our mother's womb, then why are we so afraid to trust Him? Everything we experience is all in his plan for our lives. What we do with the lessons we have learned is the key to our victories. The hardships I faced in my life have revealed to me that my gift is to have an impact on every person that I meet. I do not want to leave one life untouched. I know my calling is to serve others, to plant seeds of encouragement, hope, love, and that even just a simple smile might change the trajectory of someone's life.

I Was Born for This

"Surely your goodness and love will follow me all the days of my life, and I will dwell in the house of the Lord forever". Psalm 23:6

Life had been pretty good to me. I am thankful to have not experienced any tragedy, but I had many scars that I hadn't dealt with. The decisions that my father made in his life affected me in ways I would never speak about until many years later, before his death. Many times, as a young woman, I felt that he was just a family friend and I often thought if he were to leave this earth, I would be numb and not feel anything. Not long after I married my husband, I came to terms with him being an absent father and I decided that I would never ask him for anything again. This was to avoid the disappointment that came from the expectation of him one day changing and being a good father. Then there were the lingering effects of the negative experiences I encountered growing up being teased, sometimes bullied, and let us not forget about the church experience.

Christians avoid the fact that the church is supposed to be a place of love and healing, not retribution, judgment, and punishment. I was angry, although I knew in my heart that the church could be a good thing. God was a God of grace and mercy, not fear and bondage. So why did I not feel close to the Lord? Why did I feel that I was not worthy of his love? I don't think I understood what love is until well into my late 30s and by then, I had been married for almost fifteen years. I had a wonderful husband and two loving daughters, but something was still missing. Even though I was a member of a local church and had been since moving to Georgia in 1992, I still did not know my purpose for life. I remember, very succinctly, reading a book by a well-known author who had written a story about a woman who felt that she had wasted so much of her life – marriage, awesome family, and a successful career – but was still very unhappy. She decided to leave it all for peace of mind. It was at that moment, when I turned the last page of the book, that I realized what plans the Lord had for me in my life. Imagine, at the age of 42, my life was interrupted by words on a page in a book. Know that it is never too late to realize your purpose, of what God has called you to do in this life.

In 2005, I decided to finish my college education and I received my degree in December 2010. I wanted to be an example for my daughters so that they would know that they could do whatever they set their minds to, especially getting a higher-level education beyond high school. I always told them that education is something that no one can ever take away from you, so getting a degree is important.

While I was attending night school, my entire purpose for life came to fruition. It was no mishap that the school that I attended only had a limited number of majors that you could receive an undergraduate degree in. My choices were limited, so I selected Human Services as my degree track. By this time, I had been working for the government in the Education and Human Resources field for almost 20 years. It was during my first year in college that I would discover my heart's passion and calling in life. I knew that my gift was to help others. The one thing that kept resonating with my spirit was my mother always telling my siblings and me, that when God blesses you, you must always bless others.

Matthew 5:13-16 (MSG) *"Let me tell you why you are here. You're here to be salt-seasoning that brings out the God-flavors of this earth. If you lose your saltiness, how will people taste godliness? You've lost your usefulness and will end up in the garbage. Here's another way to put it: You're here to be light, bringing out the God-colors in the world. God is not a secret to be kept. We're going public with this, as public as a city on a hill. If I make you light-bearers, you don't think I'm going to hide you under a bucket, do you? I'm putting you on a light stand. Now that I've put you there on a hilltop, on a light stand—shine! Keep open house; be generous with your lives. By opening to others, you'll prompt people to open up with God, this generous Father in heaven."*

Let me tell you when you know that God has placed a significant calling on your life, there is nothing or no one that can stop you. Whatever the Lord has called you to do, just do it even if you are scared. Remember the strength is in the struggle.

I Have Arrived

So here I am, a fifty-two-year-old mother of two successful adult daughters, and the wife of a wonderful man. I'm a confident, successful woman that has realized that my strength was in every struggle that I have encountered. If it were not for my struggles, I would not know that the strength I needed to weather the storms of life was inside of me. However, I, too, must remember that God's promises are still true. He will never leave me nor forsake me. I have not always made the best decisions in life, but I have learned to just live in the moment of my journey. We must live in an honest way where we can be transparent to others, let them see our journey, hear our stories, know our failures, and this way, they will know that they are not alone and that their strength is in the struggle.

ABOUT THE AUTHOR

Mia Colemon is the Management and Program Analyst for the Department of Veterans Affairs in the National Cemetery Administration (NCA) in Atlanta, GA. Ms. Colemon's duties include a cadre of Human Resources responsibilities, staffing, performance appraisal, disciplinary actions, labor and employee relations, and Administrative Investigative Boards. She is the Minority Veterans Program Coordinator and the Local Reasonable Accommodation Coordinator.

Ms. Colemon is also a Certified Life Coach and an alumna of Shorter University (Class of 2010), where she received her Bachelor of Science Degree in Human Services. She believes in practicing the spirit of giving back and paying it forward, and therefore enjoys volunteering in her community. She has served on her Homeowners Association board of directors for over 10 years.

Ms. Colemon currently resides in Locust Grove, Georgia with her husband William and their two adult daughters. Her two-year-old grandson Ethan is her heartbeat.

CHAPTER 9

Tired Of Me

by Ashley Brittney

"For his anger lasts only a moment, but his favor lasts a lifetime; weeping may stay for the night, but rejoicing comes in the morning." Psalm 30:5 (NIV)

One morning, I woke up, my feet hit the ground, and I walked into my bathroom. Walking past my mirror, I caught a glimpse of myself, stopped, and began to look into my eyes. A wave of emotions rushed over me and tears started to flow rapidly down my face. I was not happy, peace was distant, joy was nowhere to be found, and I was saddened by what stared back at me. The window to my soul revealed pain, sadness, bitterness, unforgiveness, guilt, and shame, to say the least. I was staring into the face of a crushed spirit and brokenness had become my identity. "How did I get to this place? Why am I not good enough? What's wrong with me?" I questioned myself. As the tears began to overtake me, I fell to the floor burying my face in my hands, and with all of the strength I could muster, I murmured, "Lord, please help me, I am tired of being me."

What seemed like hours were only minutes as my body laid in a fetal position on my cold bathroom floor. My life flashed before my eyes as I vividly saw visions of me ending the life that was so graciously given to me. "God, where are you? I know you see me. I know you hear me." I whispered. In a puddle of tears, all that remained was the sound of silence and the darkness that hovered over me. My mind began to viciously attack me, and unwanted thoughts ran rampant in my head. I had officially lost the power to control my mind; the very thing I had prayed to keep all the days of my life, I was losing. Vivid images sent me back on a journey into my childhood and sorrow filled my heart. My soul shook as I envisioned the faces of individuals who were close to my heart, but had broken my heart, without remorse. My heart reminded me of the people whom I had poured my all into, but they did not do the same for me. I wept as I thought of the pain I was still harboring from decades past.

Moments later, I would be reunited with my 10-year-old self, standing in a doorway, as I secretly observed tears falling from the eyes of the woman who had given birth to me. Down into my bones, I experienced the pain that seeped deep down into her soul. She exuded pure beauty, dignity, integrity, and an aura of strength and courage rested upon her. Born from my mother's womb, I wondered why I didn't inherit her strength, her courage, her will to let go, and to push forward. In my spirit, I continued to carry what she had chosen to give away. As I laid there in my grief, I began to hear the melodies she would sing from the deepest part of her heart, " Tell me what do you do, when you have done all you can and it seems like it's never enough. You just stand. When there is nothing else to give, you just stand and watch the Lord see you through, and after you've done all you can, you just stand," she would sing. My mother's voice touched my ears in my darkest hour and I thought of the courage it took for her to lift her voice to The King in the face of the enemy. Pieces of my heart continued to break as I thought of how hard I tried to fit in with people who did not accept me. "Why don't I fit in? What is so wrong with my reserved nature? Why is it not okay for me to be comfortable being alone?" I thought. Tears were shed as I received myself as inadequate in the eyes of those I was so desperately trying to please. From my childhood into adulthood, even I received myself as not enough.

Everything I had prayed for in this life was mine: a husband, a child, a home, and a good job were my reality, but something was missing. For the life of me, I could not understand why happiness was like a foreign language to me. Flooding the floor, once more, were streams of tears that flushed from my face. My home was a battleground and those whom God had joined in holy matrimony were now being tested.

As if in a movie, I watched my 12-year-old-self praying, all alone in a room full of stuffed animals. Amidst a broken home, I was praying for my future home to be united. "God, please don't let me have a baby by someone I won't marry and God, please give me a marriage that will last," I prayed, as I sat there with my eyes closed and my hands clenched together. Now, as a wife, my fears and my ancient prayers were staring me dead in the face.

Laying on my plush pillow in my one-bedroom apartment, my 20-year-old face appeared to me. The prayers I had prayed over the man that would take my hand, whom I had not yet seen, were brought back into my remembrance. Those prayers began to haunt me as I was still holding on to what I believed God had joined. "God, did you hear me? What about those prayers I prayed in my innocence? Did you forget about them?" I spoke silently to him. Conflict arose between what I knew to be the power of The Almighty and what I could see in the natural world. The what-ifs of life were starting to take the lead, instead of the promises of God. Broken promises had shaped my world, not only in my past but now, in my adult life. Happily, and with great detail, my racing mind would quickly remind me of my lack of self-control, my need for control, and my inability to communicate effective-ly. As a wife, I was failing, my pride was being challenged, and humility was setting in. Guilt and shame had a grip on me and as a result, any peace I carried was being snatched away.

The God that I envisioned in the clouds when I was a child was not the God I knew. The God I served would not leave me alone like this. "God, how could you allow all these things to happen to me? I know you saw them coming." I said, breaking down again in tears. Drowning in the pain of my life, I became angry with God. My mind was shutting down on my God, but my heart was refusing to walk out.

"For I know the plans I have for you," declares the Lord, "plans to prosper you and not to harm you, to give you hope and a future." Jeremiah 29:11 (NIV)

Like a wounded soldier waiting to be rescued and taken to safety, there I was waiting to be saved. While I lay there, a little hand gently touched my shoulder and a small voice followed saying, "Mom, Mom, I'm hungry." When I turned and looked, an expression of love, concern, and sadness was visible on the face of my child. Instantly, I was taken back to the moments in time when, as a child, I shared his emotion. I empathized with my son's feelings all too well and my heart ached for him. In his innocence, he was now experiencing the very thing I had tried so hard to shield him from. "Ok, Junior, give me just a minute," I reassured him. Sitting there with my head hanging down, the pressure increased. My heart was heavy, my spirit worn; I was fragile, and my hope was lost. I struggled to find my mind to think, the strength to rise, and the words to pray. I was losing the battle.

Picturing the look on my son's face moments before, made my body curl up into a ball and I drifted further into a place of defeat. Suddenly, a small voice sprung up from my spirit, "Get up! Open those blinds. It's not over, you still have a life to live, and I will never leave you or forsake you." The spirit of The Living God had spoken, breathing the breath of life into my soul. In a millisecond everything shifted as his words begin to echo within me. My help had arrived. My Lord and Savior, the one I had prayed to, the one I believed in, had shown himself to me again in my agony. The same God that had met me for the first time on my bedroom floor in college and said He would never leave or forsake me, had stepped in again. No longer was I stranded, no longer was I searching, no longer was I lost. I had been found. The strength that I saw resting on the face of my mother started to swell up in my soul and a fight permeated my bones. When the Savior of the world spoke, I stood up, pulled back those blinds, wiped away my tears, and went to feed my son. At that moment, I was reminded that I was created to fight because

He was with me. Something was about to shift because I was certain that I was not living this life alone. Even then, I was still unsure of who I was, and I did not understand his plan or purpose for my life, but I was about to find out.

"Love the Lord your God with all your heart and with all your soul and with all your mind." Matthew 22:37 (NIV)

"Little girl, what's the greatest commandment?" my grandfather asked, with a serious look on his face while questioning his 15-year-old granddaughter. Feeling bothered by being quizzed on a Saturday afternoon as I sat on his freshly polished stairway, I replied, "I don't know Big Daddy, what is it?" His eyes pierced me as if there was nothing else in this world more important than what he was about to reveal. The truth he would speak next would be the most important part of my existence. A Saturday evening bible quiz would be a crucial part of my transformation and healing in the years to come. The spiritual glue that I needed to keep me in check for the rest of my days was about to be handed over to me. My grandfather, Claude Elliott, was about to lay a foundation of wisdom on me; he was getting ready to plant a seed. He was preparing to speak life into me so that long after he was gone, the word of God would sprout up in my soul. I would later be reunited again with my grandfather's voice ringing in my ears and through this conversation, I would find my way back to God in my darkest moments. The truth was on the tip of his tongue and once the truth was exposed it would be the answer to a plethora of questions that I would later ask God. "Love the Lord your God with all of your heart, with all of your soul and with all of your mind," he said. Seven years later, his voice echoed in my ear.

The seed that my grandfather had planted was sprouting within me. Although I had been given all the things I had prayed for, I realized all of it was nothing without God. Everything I needed was in him; he was my answer.

"I am the vine; you are the branches. If you remain in me and I in you, you will bear much fruit; apart from me you can do nothing." John 15:5 (NIV)

Desiring God had become the motivation and driving force of my life. Uncertain of how I would make it up a turbulent mountain of change, I was confident that God would be my pilot. The road would be treacherous with distractions on each side as my fleshly desires would do battle with my Spirit-filled life in Christ. The hills would be rugged and I would stumble, but I was determined to stay in the fight. Going back to who I was yesterday would not be an option. "I AM A FIGHTER!" I declared as I walked through my home. As I began to pray, I grew angry in the face of the enemy as I realized how many years had been stolen from me. I was tired of living life my way because my way was not working. I was tired of going through the cycles of life and I was done with not loving myself. God had graced me with authority through him at the beginning of creation to speak victory over my storms, and that authority was igniting my spirit. My prayers became bold with passion and authority as the spirit of God flowed through me. His words began to shut the mouth of the enemy. My Father brought out boldness and confidence in me and I was convinced that God would bring complete healing and restoration in everything that concerned me.

Change was on the horizon, and the time had come for me to suit up spiritually and put on the full armor of God. Preparing for battle meant fighting for my relationship with Christ no matter what it might cost me. It was time for me to put my Lord in his rightful place. My soul's mission was to chase after my first love, the very part of my being that was missing like a piece of a puzzle. The need to 'FIT IN" would no longer be my cross to carry. Things were changing and I desperately needed a foundation, a protector, a provider, a safe place – a place of peace, a strong tower, a companion, and a confidant. My heart yearned to be pleasing in the eyes of the Father. A brighter future filled with unexpected moments that I would not even begin to fathom was what I hoped for. To see God's promises for my life spring forward before my eyes like the promises of Abraham and Jacob is what I was believing for. The same God that raised Lazarus from his grave was the same God that would raise me out of mine. My spirit was dead and needed to be revived, and I was headed to the doctor's office. My healing was on the table, my hope was waiting to be redeemed, my peace was waiting on me to pursue it, and while I was at it, I planned to snatch up my identity.

"And we know that in all things God works for the good of those who love him, who have been called according to his purpose." Romans 8:28 (NIV)

The time had come for me to peel off the mask and get down into the heart of who I was designed to be. Developing a relationship with The King was the only way I would find out. My idea of who I thought I was and how other people viewed me was now a part of my past. The Father's thoughts towards me were my only concern and I was eager to hear what he had to say. He created me to be more than just another pretty face; I had a heart on the inside. A heart that was good, thoughtful, and caring. I was still the young girl who had a tender heart. I was still the young woman who cared for hurting people, but somewhere they both got lost in the bitterness and pain of living. Challenging God at his word, I asked him to change the heart of this broken and wounded warrior. "Deal with me first, change me, even if nothing else in my circumstances change, and see me as pleasing in your sight," I cried out to him. My destiny was on the line and the need to break the generational curses of my family rested greatly upon my spirit. My son's family was connected to me and if God chose to break the curses of my life, then the chains would be broken off his family. My mind was set on the things I could not see rather than the things I could. What I could see with my natural eyes was no hope at all, but I chose to believe there was something better that God was keeping safe just for me and my family.

The word of God, worship, fellowship, and praise with my Lord would now be the blueprint of my life. Watching the time on the clock and finding hiding places at work to pray had become my new normal. "It's eight o'clock, Father, I am coming," I would say to myself, as I snuck away like a schoolgirl to be in his presence. Occasional prayer calls would override my 30-minute lunch breaks. My first meal of the day would be the Bread of Life, at noon he would be what I thirsted for, and in the wee hours of the night, I would bow before him in spirit and truth. Closed doors at home during prayer and worship time would be considered "Mom, Mom" time and the code for Do Not Enter. Trading my cell phone for my bible would be my conversation and dates by the water would be what I looked forward to. I sought after his heart all day long and when I could not hear his voice in my heart I waited patiently. I gave him all I was able to give in worship and even in those times I still didn't feel worthy enough to stand before him. "God, create in me a pure heart," I prayed, and with each prayer, the chains that kept me bound were shattering in the face of my enemy. Even in my guilt and shame, his spirit walked with me through the fire of my emotions. Over time, he began to take away the stony heart and he created a heart of flesh and revived my spirit. The more I chased after him, the more my identity began to be shaped by his character. I was growing to love me because he loved me. Through his word, he gently corrected me, helped me, taught me, and showed me exactly who I was created to be. My Father began to expose the root cause of my pain and as I followed him, he reassured me that healing and restoration were on the way. "Lord, when I turn my face from you, pull me back to you," I prayed.

From that moment on, every morning upon my waking, he would put a song in my heart as a reminder to stay focused. "Seek my Kingdom," he would say to my heart. I began to ask him to re-move people from my life who were not a part of his plan and he replaced them with Earthly Angels filled with his power and his glory. They spoke life into me, motivated me, uplifted me, and without a doubt, I was certain that he had heard my prayer. As I began to get connected with my Earthly Angels, I found a place to belong. When I struggled in my walk, his spirit would rest upon me, and he encouraged me to stay in the fight and to trust in him. Little nuggets would drop down from heaven and into my spirit through sermons that spoke to my current situa-tion. The more I chased after him, the more he made it known to me that he was near. He began to show me glimpses of my future, and people began to speak it, confirming what he had already spoken into my heart. We had formed a bond; we were a team, and I had a partner. At 33 years old, I was about to make the most important decision of my life, yet again.

"I want to be baptized," I declared as I called the office of Tabernacle International Church. "Ok," the receptionist replied as she proceeded to tell me the date, the time, and what to wear for the ceremony. At 10 years old, I would accept Christ as my Lord and Savior but this time it held a much deeper meaning. With no doubt in my mind, I was declaring that my Lord would be the center of my life. I was declaring that I would love him with all my heart, with all my soul, and with all my mind. I was making a declaration that nothing would come before him, and I promised I would never go back to who I used to be. When the days seemed hard and tears fell from my face and onto his feet, he transformed my weakness into strength. My soul mate had found me, and I was surrounded by his love, his safety, and his security.

"Be strong and courageous. Do not be afraid or terrified because of them, for the LORD your God goes with you; he will never leave you nor forsake you." Deuteronomy 31:6 (NIV)

One morning, I woke up, my feet hit the ground, and I walked into my bathroom. As I walked past my mirror, I caught a glimpse of myself and I stopped and gazed into my eyes. For the first time, I smiled, as tears began to trickle down my cheeks. The woman I recognized in the mirror was not the same person that I once knew. I was becoming the essence of strength, confidence, boldness, and truth. Peace, love, and compassion had become my identity and I was being transformed while in the presence of God. God was replacing my sorrow with joy and my pain had been traded with his peace. The ashes were being removed and traded for the beauty that He had created in me. For the first time, I had fallen in love with me because I knew who resided within me.

I began to shine like a diamond and people could see the glory of God's light shining through me. In him, I started to gain confidence knowing that I had been made to be more than enough. Even in my mistakes, he taught me that I am not the guilt or the shame that I once carried on my shoulders. My God helped me to understand that the hurt others had inflicted on me was out of their pain and they were also in need of healing. In his presence, he helped me to see that my struggles were set up for his purpose. Without the sufferings of this world, I could have never written this story. I would not be able to encourage and motivate you to keep God first, above all things, and to NEVER EVER give up. There is beauty on the other side of every trial and sometimes we must wait just a little longer to experience the victory that awaits us.

My Savior helped me to understand that no one is perfect, and we all fall short of his glory, but he has already paid the price, so we are worthy of love. We, as human beings, are not designed to carry our burdens. 1 Peter 5:7 tells us to, "Give all your worries and cares to God, for he cares about you." At my lowest point, through all my mistakes, the Lord was still faithful and stepped into my situation and began to change in me what I could not. The death of Jesus on that old rugged cross canceled all of our guilt, shame, bitterness, and all of the other things that we choose to hold on to, but we must remember we have to step into a place of humility and make the choice to give it to him. Isaiah 53:5 tells us, "He was pierced for our transgressions, he was crushed for our iniquities; the punishment that brought us peace was on him and by his stripes, we are healed." Without pressure, breaking, and crushing in our lives, we would never be able to experience God's power, his goodness, and his faithfulness to us. My Lord showed me that there is great strength in weakness because it is where we experience his power. Although this part of my journey is not complete and my story is yet to be finished, I am confident that I will see victory and restoration in everything that concerns me. I encourage you to choose to believe in the best of what God has for you because with God on your side, you WILL NOT fail and that is a promise.

So, as I stood facing my mirror, I said, "Lord, I thank you for your love, your compassion, your forgiveness, your sweet mercy, your grace, your correction, and all that you have given to and for me." Overwhelmed with joy and peace, a smile crept back upon my face and I whispered, "Father, thank you so much for helping me find you so that I could find me." My Father whispered back into my heart saying, "Just don't forget about me."

ABOUT THE AUTHOR

Ashley Brittney was born and raised in the small towns of Hartselle and Decatur, Alabama. Ashley later went on to attend Wallace State Community College to study Occupational Therapy and she has touched the lives of many seniors as a result. Years later, Ashley's passion would blossom into the desire to touch the lives of hurting people of all ages. Through her personal experiences, Ashley was led into the field of life coaching, and she earned her Certified Life Coaching Certification from Georgia Certified Life Coaching Academy.

Ashley uses her voice and her testimonies to encourage and motivate those who are experiencing brokenness. She speaks from her heart and is eager to let those who are troubled know that they are not alone in this world. She firmly believes and testifies that God provides a way out of every situation when we diligently seek Him. Ashley is confident that we were built by God to handle any struggles we will face, and we are made stronger and more resilient because of affliction. Ashley's motto is to look up, do not give up, and stay in the fight because you will see the victory.

www.ashleybrittney.com
www.divinepurposelifecoaching.com

CHAPTER 10

I Knew Nothing About Strength Until I Found Mine

by Detral Williams

Igrew up on Main Street in a neighborhood called Skinner Town, in a small town in Central Georgia, population, approximately 5,172. I lived there with my parents and my older sister. My dad, being the head of our household, was strict. He worked as an insurance agent with the Atlanta Life Insurance Company and my mother worked as a nursing assistant, although they are both retired. Our family attended Annis Chapel Baptist Church where my dad served as a deacon and the superintendent of the Sunday school class. My mom taught the Beginners

Sunday school class. My parents worked day and night so that my sister and I could have the best in life. I remember my dad coming home around lunchtime on Saturday and I would run out to his car and ask, "Daddy, can I drive?" I would jump in his lap and twist the steering wheel while he would press the gas pedal in the car, and I was so excited because I was driving. I must admit that my sister and I were spoiled, but it was a good spoil. I thank God that we never had to experience not having enough.

My dad had two other children before he and my mom were married. My half-sister didn't live in the same city as we did, so we didn't know about her until one day my dad invited us to go to a wedding. My mom, my sister who was in high school, and I, who was in middle school, were sitting in the church wondering where's Daddy when the church doors opened and to our surprise, who was walking the bride down the aisle but my daddy. My sister and I turned to our mother and asked, "Who is she?" The look on my mother's beautiful face was one of hurt, pain, and deceit.

As a little girl, I felt my mother's pain, and I still didn't have a clue about what was going on, but because she appeared hurt, I was hurt. It seemed as if our whole world as a family had changed forever. I love my mother dearly, but in my eyes, my daddy could do no wrong. We never knew that Daddy had another child. Our brother lived in the same hometown that we did, and we see him all the time and are very close, but I still had a hard time in the past accepting him as my brother. I always thought our family should have been only me, Mom, Dad, and my sister. I was very selfish. I didn't realize the effect of rejecting my dad's kids had a great impact on them.

Attending high school was one of the best, most fun times of my life. I met my high school sweetheart, who was the captain of the football team when I was in 10th grade and he was in 12th grade. Whenever the football team had a home game and won, they were treated to a steak dinner and the players could bring a guest, so as his girlfriend, I was right there with him. We also went to the prom together and I was so excited to go to the prom with a Senior! It was a great privilege for me to go because, at our school, we had to be a Junior to attend prom. After my boyfriend graduated from high school and went off to college, we continued to date. I worked and attended a Junior College, and when he came home on the weekend, we would go to the movies, out to eat, and ride around town holding hands, while he was driving a stick shift car. We were so in love!

After my boyfriend graduated from college, he joined the army. His first assignment was in Korea...yes, Korea. I was so heartbroken that my boyfriend and best friend were leaving me. I was so lonely although we did keep in touch by writing letters weekly and talking on the telephone. Oh, my God, there were times when the telephone bill got up to $500.00, and our parents were livid. We were working but back then, I was only making minimum wage and I remember that several times, I had to give my entire check to my father for a telephone bill. I am so thankful that I was still living at home with my parents. While my boyfriend was serving time in Korea, he proposed to me over the telephone after I received my engagement ring by mail. Of course, he tells a different story. He says that it was only supposed to be a friendship ring, but when he came home on military leave, he ended up at the wedding shop, trying on a tuxedo. He always tells the story like that and to this day, he is sticking to it.

On November 12, 1994, one of the happiest days of my life, I married my best friend and high school sweetheart. Standing at the altar in his tuxedo, waiting to take my hand in marriage, he took my breath away. After the wedding, we left to go on our honeymoon, but we didn't go too far away because the next week we were leaving to start our new life together as husband and wife in Fort Huachuca, Arizona. It was a long, three-day road trip, but we enjoyed each other's company. When we arrived at our new duty station it was so different from home. I had been asleep and remember waking up saying, "Is this it?" My husband looked at me and replied, "Baby, I'm so sorry." It was okay though because I made up my mind that day that I was going to make the best out of it. There was nothing in Arizona except dirt, cacti, and dead grass. There were no restaurants or hair salons and we had to drive an hour to go to the mall. However, once we got settled into our new place and found our routine, it wasn't so bad. I began to make new friends. We had family come out to visit us, we drove to Dallas, Texas to visit friends, and we also drove out to Las Vegas, twice. Believe it or not, I was beginning to enjoy the desert life. After spending three years in the Arizona desert, it was time to come back to Georgia as my husband had received military orders to move to Augusta.

Upon arriving at the base in Fort Gordon, it felt so refreshing to be back in Georgia as we were only three hours away from family. I was home just about every weekend and on holidays. Living in Augusta was nice because we had everything we needed. My husband and I loved eating out, and we had a variety of restaurants to choose from, a hairdresser for me to get my hair done, and we went to comedy shows. Life was good! I worked full-time at the hospital and decided to take night classes. I loved my job working for an Indian doctor, and once a week she would take me and my coworker out to eat at her Indian restaurant. It took a while to get used to but I began to like Indian food. I didn't try to make new friends in Augusta though, because I knew we were only there for a short time. After spending a year at Fort Gordon, it was time to move again and this time it was far, far away, to Germany. I was sad, but at the same time, I was happy because I was about to embark on a whole new experience. I was flying to another country I had never been to before. Once we received orders to move to Baumholder, Germany, we had two weeks to get there. We had to make sure that we had our passports, our car had to be shipped, movers had to come and pack up our belongings, and we had to say goodbye to everyone. Once we arrived at the airport, I knew there was no turning back, not that I wanted to.

Once we arrived in Frankfurt, Germany, we had a driver pick us up and take us to our location. It was cold and raining, we were at the wrong post, and it was late. We had no idea where to go or who to talk to. We had to wait there until another set of orders were written up and sent down before we were able to go to another post. My husband kept apologizing to me for how sorry he was that they messed up his orders. I had to let him know that it was okay and that it wasn't his fault at all. As long as I was with my husband, I knew we were going to be okay and that he was going to take care of me.

We received orders around 1:00 a.m. and we went to our room which was in the barracks where single soldiers lived. My husband had met a couple of guys that night and they invited him to watch the Super Bowl game with them. By this time, I was sick with a sore throat and cough so I slept on the top bunk and I let my husband have the bottom bunk. The next day we left, and they put us up in a German hotel until housing was available.

We were still without a car, when one day, we went to the commissary (military grocery store) and as we came out of the store with bags in our hands, most certainly looking lost, a guy asked if we needed a ride. We immediately jumped in the car with a stranger and he took us back to the hotel.

Once we got housing and I learned my way around, I met new friends and we exchanged telephone numbers. I joined a church, which was quite different from the one I had attended in the United States, and started working at Baumholder School-Age Services. It was a before and after-school program where parents would drop their kids off at 5:00 a.m. and pick them up by 6:00 p.m. I worked in the office as an After-school Coordinator and I enjoyed my job. It was always interesting to hear how the kids' day went at school. They all had a story to tell. I remember two little twin girls who loved Ms. Dee. Every day, before and after school, they would always give me a big hug. They even had their parents calling me Ms. Dee.

Another good thing about living in Germany was one of my best friends that I grew up with was already living there with her family. She showed me around and taught me how to exchange US currency for German money. I did a lot of traveling while living in Germany. I got a chance to visit Italy, Paris, France, Poland, and my husband and I also attended the Oktoberfest Festival in Munich.

As I started to settle into my new lifestyle in Europe, I would notice things that were different than what I was used to in the United States. When we went out to a restaurant, we would ask for water. It might have been cold from being in the refrigerator but they didn't serve ice with our drinks. The waiter would offer us bread, along with condiments, before serving our meals and when we received the bill, the water and bread had been added on. I guess that was a European thing. We also had to pay to use the public restroom, so make sure if you travel to Europe you have 50 cents to use their toilet because someone will be sitting at the door collecting money. Oh my God, I am so terrified of dogs. People would be walking their dogs with no leashes on them or you might see a dog walking by itself, although it wasn't a stray. I must admit that they were very well-trained, so I discovered there was nothing to worry about. They were allowed just about everywhere, including at the mall and in restaurants. I had to get used to this because I am not a dog lover and I wasn't used to dogs being allowed in places where people eat, but they were well-behaved.

The legal drinking age in Georgia is 21. I remember my husband and I walked into a restaurant and saw a kid who looked like he could have been a teenager, sitting at the bar drinking a beer. They didn't check ID unless you were on the military base. Germany offered free education and the thought of having to pay back student loans for years was completely foreign to them.

After spending eight years in the army, my husband decided it was time to get out. His father used to tell him all the time that he thought he would stay in the military and become a General. How I wished he would have stayed to become a General. Instead, he decided to go back to school full-time to get his Master of Business Administration (MBA) degree. I was somewhat sad because in the military we were all one, big, happy family. Transitioning from military life to civilian life was challenging for me. When we flew back to Stateside, we drove from Atlanta to Eastman, which is a three-hour drive, but it seemed like it took us forever to get home. The drive wasn't bad. I was anxious to see my family and friends. We spent two weeks at home before embarking on our next journey together.

We had talked about making Memphis our home and at this point, we finally settled down in a place that felt like home.

However, after spending a year in Memphis, one day my mom called me to tell me that my dad had been acting strangely and wasn't himself. I asked her what she meant and she told me that he was starting to forget a lot of stuff that he shouldn't. My husband knew that I was my daddy's girl so I didn't have to say a word and he started making plans to get me closer to home to be with my family. I will be forever grateful and love him for that.

My mom made doctor's appointments and they kept saying they couldn't find anything wrong with Dad. We finally took him to a neurologist who told us that my dad was in the first stage of Alzheimer's and all I could think was the doctors are wrong… not my daddy. He had never been sick or needed to go to the doctor. My daddy was always the strong one who took care of his family, and we had never wanted for anything. We decided to leave the Home of the Blues to be with family.

Before leaving Memphis, we decided that McDonough, Georgia would be our home. We knew we didn't want to be too close or too far away from family. My husband started his new job and I started working at Curves Fitness Center. However, I found a church home in McDonough, made new friends, and still have friends there from before I got married.

We found out that I was pregnant two weeks after arriving in McDonough and were so excited, we decided to tell everybody on Mother's Day. Everyone received a Mother's Day card in which we had placed the ultrasound picture, and when they opened it up, they saw that we were having twins. But on Father's Day, I was standing at the altar at church for prayer and I felt a flutter. A couple of weeks later, I had a miscarriage. We were heartbroken.

It was good to be settled in Georgia where I was close enough to be able to check on my dad. I called home every day, sometimes two and three times a day. I also started taking night classes at Clayton State University and I recall one night, I was on my way home and I was listening to the radio and a song came on. It was called "Let Go and Let God." At this point, I was getting angry with God. When I got home, I sat in my car crying, screaming at God, asking him, "Why my daddy? God, my daddy has always taken care of his family, he has never missed church, and he kept me and my sister in the church. He paid his tithes and offerings faithfully. He worked hard so that we didn't have to suffer. He helps people along the way, and this is how you repay my daddy…by making him suffer?" I told God that I did not want any part of this Christian life. And then, during my crying, screaming, and questioning God, I heard God say to me, "Your daddy is alright, he's good. I'm trying to bring y'all closer to me." At that moment, all I could say was, "Okay." I surrendered. After having that encounter with God, I stopped calling home three and four times a day and every time I talked with my mother, I stopped asking how Daddy was doing.

We had a family reunion in Detroit, Michigan, and as we were getting ready to tour Detroit, I helped my sister get my dad to the restroom before we got on the bus. Dad had no control of himself when he had to go to the restroom, and when I realized this, I lost it. I cried uncontrollably as I had never seen my daddy helpless. He had gotten to a point where he couldn't do anything for himself anymore, although I was in denial about this for at least the first two or three years of his disease. It was so hard for me. I needed my daddy and I was worried that if I didn't go home on the weekend or if I missed a holiday, it might be my last holiday with him. I had to realize that I had no control. I couldn't change the fact that my daddy was sick, and he was, for many years.

I thank God for my beautiful mother. She took care of my daddy and took him to the best doctors. She made sure that he continued to go to church, and whenever we went on trips, he was always right there with us. I never heard my mother complain about taking care of him. My mother honored her vows, in sickness and in health, till death do us part. I thank God for covering my mother in strength.

When I went home to visit, I made sure that I went by to check on my mother-in-law, who was a special lady in my life. If I didn't go to her house, I would always meet her at Sunday School. I did this to validate the special bond that we had. My mother-in-law was also my high school homeroom teacher.

I started working full-time and enjoyed my job at the hospital. I have been working in the medical field for over 20 years. However, in 2015 my husband was laid off from his job and this began to put a strain on our marriage. I noticed he was becoming depressed. He was constantly applying for jobs and would have interviews but no one would call him back for employment. He started avoiding family and friends and didn't want to talk to anyone. We started drifting further and further apart and our communications became extremely limited. I tried talking to him, asking, "What can I do to help?" He always told me that he was okay, for me to go and enjoy my life. I suggested that maybe we should seek counseling but he declined. I asked myself if maybe I should have kept pushing him, but that is not who I am. I respect a person's space when they want to be left alone. He told me that I couldn't fight his demons although I tried for many years because I loved him. He became emotionally abusive and was always agitated. Everything was my fault and he looked at me as if he hated my guts. I constantly asked him to name one thing that I did to him and he could never tell me. He was not the same person that I had fallen in love with. I hated coming home after work so I would go to the park and just sit there until dark. I also got a second job at night so that we would have extra income but felt as if my life was out of control and I didn't know which way to turn or who to turn to.

I called Friday my wine down. I would stop by the store and get two bottles of wine to carry me through Friday and Saturday, just to numb the hurt and take away the stress. I did not drink on Sunday, because I was in church and surrounded by people and was receiving the word of God.

Also in 2015, I was diagnosed with breast cancer in my left breast. I remembered sitting in the Emergency room with my sister and cousin because my dad had to be rushed to the ER for treatment. While there, my doctor called to give me the results of my mammogram. He told me that I had stage 0 cancer. I thought, okay, does that mean there is no cancer? He said, "Oh, you have cancer, it's just not outside of the lining." My world stopped. I went from being worried about my dad lying in the ER bed not knowing what was going on with him, to this. My first thought was, oh my God, I could die. I told my doctor, "I can't take all this in, I need to call my husband," so while my doctor explained everything to my husband on the telephone, my husband was on his computer at the house doing research. When I got home, he sat me down and explained everything to me. He was with me every step of the way. I felt safe and was sure that everything was going to be alright, and as always, he took exceptionally good care of me. As of July 5, 2020, I am cancer-free. I am a survivor!

After going through breast cancer, a few years later I lost two people that were near and dear to my heart. In November 2017, my mother-in-law passed away and in December of that year, my dad passed. I was numb, in shock, full of rage, angry, and sad. I was lonely and felt like I had no one to talk to in this big world. My husband couldn't comfort me because he was hurting himself. When we encountered death at the same time, I thought we would get through it together and I know that we all grieve differently, but he shut down on me completely. I couldn't talk to my mom and sister, because they were going through the same pain that I was going through. I thought that I was going to lose my mind. The one person I tried talking to pretty much told me that I had to get over it, that I had to figure it out. Guess what? I did.

I guess it wasn't enough for me to have a miscarriage, breast cancer, and to lose my loved ones. I guess God was telling me, "My child you can handle this because, in the end, you are going to give me all the glory."

My dad had always made sure that my sister and I had good credit so I didn't have a clue that my husband had run up credit charges in my name until a sheriff rang my doorbell and served me papers. I was over $10,000.00 in debt. My husband didn't try to explain, all he said was that bills had to be paid. I was still trying to save my marriage and didn't know what was happening. I had to go to court to officially report that I knew nothing about the credit charges and my only option was to file charges against my husband. I thought I can't do that, he is my husband. What will people think? What will our family think? He is walking around hating me for the damage he caused. He could be in prison now, but you hate. Why?

My car was repossessed, not once but twice. The first time was on New Year's Eve when I had got off work in the morning from my night job. I went outside and thought my car had been stolen so I called the police to report it. I was so terrified. I called my husband and he told me that they probably came to pick it up. I tried for several months to pay my car note, but he kept telling me not to worry about it as he was handling it. The same day, we went to the car pound to pick up my car. I thank God that my daddy taught me the importance of saving.

The second time was while I was at my day job. I was in my office and the janitor knocked on my door and said, "Ms. Dee, I don't know what's going on, but they are taking your car." I jumped up and ran outside to find my car was already on the tow truck. There I was in the parking lot, running behind the truck. I called my husband all day but he didn't answer my telephone calls. I was so embarrassed, hurt, and felt like I had been deceived. I trusted this man. We had taken out a loan to pay the car note and the rest of the bills. So, what happened to the money? I thanked God that I was able to get my car back the next day. I had bill collectors calling me every day wanting their money. I was sick to my stomach and he told me not to answer the telephone. He did this to me on purpose, literally trying to destroy me. All I could do was pray and trust God.

In 2019, a family member offered to allow us to live in her house which I appreciated from the bottom of my heart. It would have helped us out a lot, but I wasn't going to destroy someone else's home like my home had been destroyed. I remember that we were lying in bed and he said, "I'm taking the offer to move into her house. The moving truck will be here in three days. You can come if you want to." I took it as if he was saying I didn't have to, but since we are married, it was up to me. I thought, three days and you are telling me this now. He talked about what the movers could take and what could go in storage. As we were lying in bed, he asked me if I had heard what he said. I didn't say anything because I couldn't speak. It was like I tried to open my mouth, but nothing came out. He asked me three times, and I tried to say something, but I couldn't. He jumped out of bed and he was mad. So, after he moved out, I was left to clean a five-bedroom house by myself, while working two jobs as I couldn't afford to have someone come in and clean the house for me. As I was cleaning, I kept thinking how could someone be so evil? What happened to us?

Needless to say, we separated. He took the offer to leave and I didn't go. I had never been on my own, from my parents' home to marrying my husband. I was totally lost. My family didn't know that we were separated, and I didn't have a clue about what I was going to do. I prayed, trusted God, and kept the faith. I kept praying and telling God, "I know that you have a plan for my life." I was in a very dark place for so many years. It was so easy to hide behind a fake smile. It wasn't until I surrendered to

God, fell to my knees, threw up my hands, and told God, "I give it all to you." Once I surrendered everything to God, I was free.

Despite everything that happened to me, God helped me get through it and I give him all the glory! I wasn't built to break, but to endure, persevere, and stand firm in my faith. I thanked and praised him for helping me with everything I went through, and this is why I can smile again. Be encouraged. The Lord is with those who believe and have faith.

ABOUT THE AUTHOR

Detral Williams has been serving in the healthcare field for over 20 years. She is currently employed with Well-Star Sylvan Grove Hospital in Jackson, Georgia, serving as the Business Office Coordinator. She is a Certified Revenue Cycle Representative (CRCR), and a certified Life Coach, specializing in grief and encouragement. Detral also volunteers with Emmanuel State Prison's Women's Facility, is a mentor for Women in Transition, a Court Appointed Special Advocate for Children (CASA), and a volunteer with the Georgia Firefighters Burn Foundation. She resides in McDonough, Georgia.

CHAPTER 11

Opposition from Within

by Sharon P. Jones

Hello, meet Sharon. Sharon is a daughter, sister, wife, mother, aunt, and friend. Sharon is also a soldier (retired from the military), minister, pastor's wife, football and soccer mom as well as a school volunteer. Whatever Sharon finds herself doing, she is serving with a smile. Beyond Sharon's smile, she deals with opposition from within. There are many meanings to the word opposition but the two most relevant in my life are these: "1. is the action of opposing, resisting, or combating; 2. antagonism or hostility." (Source: Dictionary.com)

Opposition from within is internalized feelings that are designed to keep one from living according to their ordained purpose. These feelings are derived from how a person truly feels about themselves on the inside. The opposition within Sharon is self-sabotage. I will provide an understanding of what self-sabotage is and how one unknowingly does this. Sabotage, as a noun, according to Dictionary.com is: "any underhand interference with production, work, etc., in a plant, factory, etc., as by enemy agents during wartime or by employees during a trade dispute; 2. any undermining of a cause." In the practical sense, self-sabotage can show up as undermining, either by being undermined or undermining oneself. When the word self is added to the word sabotage, this indicates that one is going against oneself. How does one go against oneself? One goes against oneself by or through identity issues, distraction, and time management. These elements are not all-inclusive.

To determine individual opposition from within, take some time to reflect and search within. In this search, one should be honest to determine what is causing the opposition from within. Let's take a moment of silence. In this silence, think about goals set and goals that were completed, and especially the goals that were not completed. Examine each goal that has not been completed and review the steps in the process of attaining these goals. Review each step individually and determine which ones are completed. When reviewing the ones that are not complete, honestly assess why the goal has not been completed. Once the reason is clear, look closely to determine what could have been done differently to complete the goal. Revisit the goal and persevere.

Opposition from within is triggered by an unclear identity. When one doesn't know who they are or what they were put on earth to do, there is an identity issue. This person is existing but not really living. When identity is unclear, one's purpose is also unclear.

There is not enough discussion about individual opposition from within. It is important to discuss because people are waging internal battles and the enemy does not always come from an external force. When one experiences opposition, it is easy to blame others so that one exonerates oneself. Understanding about self-sabotage is needed because so many people are unaware of this behavior. After reading for the next few minutes, one should be able to identify whether their opposition from within is due to self-sabotage or from an outside force.

I will discuss opposition from within around poor self-perception, distractions, and time management.

Poor self-perception or low self-esteem occurs because of our thoughts. This occurs when we say something negative about another person and they believe it to be true. As a little girl, I had and still have, dark skin and coarse hair. My parents divorced when I was around eight years old. As a result of the divorce, the household experienced a drastic financial change. I would often get teased and called ugly by other kids, especially boys. Over the years, I perceived this information to be true. There was harsh name-calling and I would still hear those names as I entered adulthood. As a result of being teased and called names, I lacked confidence. My self-perception had been shaped by other people's opinions and I believed them. Unchecked, untreated, poor self-perception plays out in different ways.

At a young age, I had become withdrawn. I was very quiet and shy. I wouldn't speak or greet anyone unless I was spoken to. Because I was quiet, I'd often get overlooked. This would be the start of withdrawn behavior that would continue for years. For many years I had accepted that that was who I was. As a young adult, I went to college and I always had a job. I would work hard at my job, school, and extracurricular activities, etc., and I'd get overlooked for promotions or special recognition as an individual or as a team member in a group. I was raised to work hard. I didn't work hard so that I would receive recognition, but if employees are getting recognized for whatever criteria, everyone should be recognized. Nonetheless, because I was timid, I didn't speak up or plea my case, I just took one for the team. I let things go. I remember one time in middle school (maybe 6th grade) that two boys were playing around and one of them bumped me with my lunch tray and knocked my lunch out of my hand. I just walked back to my assigned table and didn't eat lunch that day. Another incident I recall was when I was about nine years old. Our aunt would have the biggest and best holiday family gatherings and as dinner was served on this occasion, everyone had a plate except for me. I didn't say anything. I just sat at the "kid's table." While everyone was eating, my mom noticed that I didn't have a plate and fussed at me for not speaking up and letting someone know. My mom worked with me over time to learn to speak up and with her consistent help and guidance, I slowly overcame my shyness. There were still times when I was timid when I should have been vocal, but over the years, I've greatly improved. Many people in my life can verify that my being withdrawn is no longer an issue. This didn't happen overnight, it was an intentional process, and many years would pass until I was confident to both speak and speak up for myself.

In the process of overcoming shyness, I had become exposed to confidence-building exercises while in the military, and later I would attend and complete officer training. I was also surrounded by people who were positive and believed in me. With an increase in confidence, I was able to express myself and started believing in myself. I was setting goals and meeting them. Once my self-perception changed, how I felt about myself has changed. My self-perception caused opposition from within.

Opposition is also experienced in the form of distractions. According to Dictionary.com, distract is defined in the verb tense (used with object) as: "1. to draw away or divert, as the mind or attention; 2. to disturb or trouble greatly in mind; beset; 3. to provide a pleasant diversion for; amuse; entertain; 4. to separate or divide by dissension or strife." Currently, many distractions are vying for our attention. There are a plethora of distractions to deal with but for this discussion, I refer to TV, social media, the telephone, and self-aggrandizement. While writing this, three of these distractions interrupted me.

Television is self-explanatory as a distraction. Sometimes there is nothing like a good show or movie in the evening to relax with. However, there is an issue when the next show and the one after that come on and by the evening's end, no work, tasks, or assignments have been completed. Even worse, the three shows I watched were reruns and had already been seen several times. The gravity from the TV created a force that prevented an assignment from being completed and the assignment could have been anything that was scheduled for the evening (home project, laundry, writing a book chapter, etc.). Distraction from television can be hypnotizing and also detrimental to relationships because there is no human interaction taking place. The daily/evening line-up of shows can or will cause you to not want to do anything except to watch. The mind is focused on what show is coming on next. There was a movie that came out in the nineties about four women, all of whom worked. Two of the women balanced motherhood and they all enjoyed occasionally getting together. One of the characters didn't care about a social life and just wanted to stay home and watch television all night. While she would go out with her friends, her mind would drift to which rerun was on television that night; reruns that she had probably watched numerous times. I reflected on the different movies and shows that I have watched many times and yet still do not want anyone to talk to me when they are on air. My overindulgence in television to the point of not meeting or setting goals is a distraction that causes opposition from within.

Social media, for many years, has strategically entered the lives of humans and created havoc for some. In moderation, social media can be a great tool. When I first got into social media, it was to keep up with the millennials in my family. Now, social media serves as a great tool for business and business development. I get up in the morning and read daily scriptures on a Bible app and I also post the scripture on my social media page. When I am not focused, I start scrolling through the news feed, and then I see that I've spent 35-40 minutes on social media; time that would have been better spent doing something else. I still monitor the time I spend on social media in an effort to remain focused, but it is very easy to review notifications and then look up to see that 30 minutes or more have passed while scrolling. I allow overindulgence in social media to be a part of my opposition from within.

The telephone, its purpose, and its function has evolved over the years and with each generation. Who would have guessed that the telephone could be this smart? Only a select few technology insiders knew that it would evolve to what it is today. My daughter bought me a smartphone. As I got used to the phone, I noticed that it can do many things, and it tracks everything. The phone tracks habits, exercise, driving patterns, and with its applications (apps) there is so much more that a smartphone can tell you about yourself. I remember the first time I noticed that the smartphone was letting me know what time I would arrive at work depending on what time I left the house. When I first received these notifications, I was creeped out by how the phone knew my every move. When I realized this, I started exploring my phone, and then I would become distracted when it came to completing tasks and assignments. I had to be careful as the phone had started to consume more and more of my time. When I was in graduate school and was working to complete assignments, I'd start looking through my phone and would lose a significant amount of time studying due to being on social media or sometimes just reviewing apps and even games. Distractions also occur while videos pop up. How many videos are watched before we realize it is time to get back to the assignment at hand?

I'm learning more about the functionality of my current smartphone and have discovered that it serves a greater purpose. There are times that I can complete reports and conduct other business on the phone when I am unable to get to the laptop. The amount of work that can be done with a smartphone when not using an actual computer is quite amazing. My phone alerts me every Sunday morning, letting me know how many hours per day I was using/holding it during the previous week. Telephone distraction is part of my opposition from within.

Self-aggrandizement is most definitely another contributor to opposition from within. The definition of aggrandize according to Dictionary.com in the verb tense (used with object) is: "1. to widen in scope; increase in size or intensity; enlarge; extend; 2. to make great or greater in power, wealth, rank or honor; 3. to make (something) appear greater." In the practical sense, this is when someone performs a deed, and it is done with the mindset that if they do not do it, that it will not get done. How many times when you're focused, pursuing your goals, and working, does it seem like certain people draw you into their crises and expect you to help? How many times have you stopped what you were doing to aid someone in their crisis? When you've finished helping, how long did it take for you to get back on track, or was the opportunity lost?

I reflect on a time that I had committed to updating and purging my kitchen. This project was to take one week as I worked during the day and could only work on it in the evening. One of my co-workers needed a ride to and from work and as a request, it seemed pretty harmless. However, this co-worker ended up riding with me for about six weeks and her energy was draining. Every day I would be tired because I left home a little earlier so that I could be on time for work, but I would get home later after dropping her off. Sometimes, she needed to stop at the grocery store or somewhere else. My kitchen project took approximately three weeks to complete because of the lack of time I had in the evening. This affected the completion of other projects that I had lined up around the house as well. I didn't have to take my co-worker to and from work as she could have taken public transportation or other options available to her. I was concerned with making sure that she would get back and forth to work, but ultimately it was not my responsibility. I was moving into a new place, spiritually, and thought it was my responsibility to help her. A lesson to self: when helping others, determine if I am the one who must perform the job. Make sure that by providing help to others that I am not taken so off-course that I am distracted from what I should be doing. If someone calls and they are in a crisis, do not decide at that time; offer to call back after assessing my current situation. Being distracted through self-aggrandizement is why I have opposition from within.

There are too many things that compete for our time. Some of us are guilty of picking up assignments/tasks that have nothing to do with us, or our schedule. Time management or lack thereof can affect our focus. Not being focused also affects time management. Not using time wisely is an opposing factor when completing a task. Tracking and monitoring daily activities will save some time when working on a specific project. It takes a consciously organized person to maintain a daily activity journal. Over the years, I have used different methods of tracking activities. When I was younger, I would make a "must-do list" on a sheet of paper, at night as well as in the morning. I also had a similar "must-do list" on my desk at work. Another planning method that I used was simple. I liked the month-at-a-glance calendar so that I could see the entire month. On this calendar, I would type in dates like doctor's appointments for me and the children, sports activities, business meetings, school meetings, bible study, choir rehearsal, etc. I would also enter work hours and the children's school hours as well as days off. After those dates were added, I would type in the dates for projects based on personal goals, and then, at last, highlight any extra time I had left. Using this method prevented overbooking or making commitments that conflicted with what was already on the schedule. These days, I generally use a calendar/planner now with the same method. I also use the calendar and the Notes section on my smartphone. Failure to properly plan my time is part of my opposition from within.

Opposition from within is real. To move forward, I had to pray, meditate, and read the Holy Bible. I needed spiritual reinforcement because my flesh would naturally go against God's will. There are so many scriptures that have inspired me to stay focused. God's reminder to me when I'm wavering regarding my identity and self-perception is 1 Peter 2:9: "But ye are a chosen generation, a royal priesthood, an holy nation, a peculiar people; that ye should shew for the praises of him who hath called you out of darkness into his marvelous light." (KJV) God's reminder to me when I am distracted is in Romans 12:1-2: "I beseech you therefore, brethren, by the mercies of God, that ye present your bodies a living sacrifice, holy, acceptable unto God, which is your reasonable service. 2. And be not conformed to this world: but be ye transformed by the renewing of your mind, that ye may prove what is that good, and acceptable, and perfect, will of God." (KJV) Lastly, God's reminder to me regarding time management is Ecclesiastes 3:1-3: "To everything there is a season and a time to every purpose under the heaven; 2. a time to be born, and a time to pluck up that which is planted; 3. a time to kill, and a time to heal; a time to break down and a time to build up." (KJV)

This is the determination of opposition from within due to self-sabotage in the areas of self-perception, distractions, and time management. Moving forward, one must stop settling for good things when one should accept great things. Ultimately, we should expect and accept what God wants for us. In terms of self-perception or self-aggrandizement, one sabotages oneself by trying to be everything to everybody which none of us was meant to do. When it comes to distractions, one must realize and understand that one cannot be all and do all as it relates to everyone. This is not humanly possible. Lastly, regarding time management, one must be intentional about being in the right place at the right time doing the right thing. Ultimately, God is best for us.

ABOUT THE AUTHOR

Lady Sharon Jones is the CEO of Queendominion Enterprises, LLC (established 2011), and Executive Director and Founder of Women on the Front-Line Global Outreach Ministries (established November 2013). Its vision is "Transforming Lives, Impacting Generations," while its mission is to encourage, empower, and educate women of all generations to live a victorious life in Christ according to Bible scripture 3 John 2: "Beloved, I wish above all things that thou mayest prosper and be in health, even as thy soul prospereth."

Lady Sharon has earned a bachelor's degree from Queens College (Flushing, NY), a Master of Science Degree (Public Administration Concentration) from Central Michigan University, and a Graduate Certificate in Project Management from Capella University. Sharon also received a Diploma from Georgia Certified Life Coach Academy, and certificates of completion for "When Leaders Lead" taught by the late Bishop Earl Paulk from the Cathedral of the Holy Spirit and Master Life Discipleship Series.

Lady Sharon served in the U.S. Army Reserves for over 20 years and completed service at the Officer rank of Captain. Sharon has over 20 years of experience working with the Department of Human Resources/Services in New York and Georgia and is a former Business Analyst with the State of Georgia. She currently serves as a board member with Pillar of Fire Christian Ministries, in Biloxi, MS, Pathway Christian Ministries, in Atlanta, GA, and formerly with The Elect Lady Ministries, in McDonough, GA. Sharon is a Certified Life Coach and best-selling author. Lady Sharon is a New York native who has made Atlanta her home.

Facebook @wotflgobal
Facebook @Sharon Jones Author
Instagram @wotflglobal

CHAPTER 12

The Night That Changed
the Course of My Life

by Renata Triblett

It was a hot summer night in Sikeston, Missouri, in July of 1995, and I had decided that I was going to get what I wanted. So, I walked over to his mother's house and I knocked on his window. He looked out at me with a face like, what in the world! He opened the window and asked, "What are you doing here?" I replied, "I came to see you." He was hesitant for a second and then he let me in. I don't remember everything that we talked about word for word, but what I do know for a fact is that I let him know that I wanted him, and I wanted him to teach me some things. He looked at me and told me that I was one of his niece's friends and that I was too young to know what I wanted, but after a while of me persuading him, he finally gave in and gave me what I wanted.

We started to make out and as he began to take off my clothes, he stopped suddenly because he noticed that I had a sock full of money. He asked, "What are you doing with all that money?" I told him that some of it was mine, but most of it was my mom's, for bills. He was gentle with me and I had never been with anyone like him. I had never even taken a shower with anyone other than myself. That night, I said to myself, I am a woman.

Two days had passed since our meaningful encounter and the next thing I heard, he was back in prison and was going to be gone for four years. That's right, I said back in prison. You see, the first time I had ever laid my eyes on him he had just got out of prison, and I thought he was so fine. I was over at his niece's house when he walked in the door. I asked her, "Girl, who is that?" and she said, "That's my uncle." She also let me know that he was way too old for me. However, at that moment, age didn't mean a thing to me.

A few years went by and he never really paid me any attention, I was just a kid with a little crush. Then one day he noticed me. You must understand that I was getting a little older and my body was filling out my clothes. He asked me, "How old did you say you were again?" I said, "Old enough." From then until the night that I showed up at his window, we gave each other looks. He would smile at me and it would just make my day.

Time passed and that fabulous night was just a memory. It was now fall and the carnival was in town, it always came in the late summer and early fall. I was hanging out with my friends and family and we were playing games and taking amusement park rides. I remember it like yesterday, we got on this ride that you stand on and it goes in circles; I think it was called "Zero Gravity." Anyway, when I got off the ride, I was so nauseous and couldn't recover from the motion, and suddenly, I started vomiting everywhere. I thought it was from eating too much cotton candy and all those other famous foods and candies we like to eat at the carnival. Boy, was I wrong! That's right, that magical night that I enjoyed so much was the night that I conceived my first child.

I had a boyfriend at the time who was my age, and I was also sexually active with him. Oh yeah, and by the way, I was only 15 years old. Yes, that's right, I was just a baby myself. I was only 14 on the night that I was with him. I had a birthday that summer. My mother had no idea I was even having sex. I was what they call a "Fast Tail Girl" back then. It was quite normal where I'm from and it could still be going on today. I mean, you have the older guys preying on the young girls and the older women preying on the young boys.

Listen up, young girls/ladies and young boys/men. When you start to fill out your clothes and you think or feel like you know what you want, please take the time and talk to an adult to help you deal with your emotions. There is so much more to it than giving yourself or your body away. You may think you know what you want. Not too long ago, I used to blame myself for what happened to me and make excuses for my ex-husband's actions. I now know that it was wrong for him to take advantage of me, and although, yes, I approached him, he was the adult and should have declined my suggestion.

Around the time when I found out I was pregnant, my mother had just taken my older sister to the doctor because she thought she was being sexually active. My sister used to sneak out of the house with my aunt and go to the club when she thought our parents were sleeping. My mother had five girls and one boy. I was child number three. You remember earlier when I said I had a sock full of money and most of it was my mother's? Well, that goes to show you that she trusted me, and I was supposed to be the responsible one.

I thought, oh my goodness, what am I going to do now? I couldn't panic as I had to figure things out. Should I tell my boyfriend, my friends, my mom, who should I talk to? No one! I didn't tell a soul. To be honest, I didn't know if the child was my boyfriend's or the result of my one-night adventure, so I kept it to myself. I continued with my life as usual. I went to school and hung out with my friends. I had to stay productive because if I slowed down, my mother would know that something was going on.

I know you're wondering how a 14-year-old could have money. Well, since about the age of ten, I learned very quickly that you cannot have the things that you want without money. Back then, I would mow grass, rake leaves, and shovel snow to make money. Nowadays, a lot of kids feel entitled and believe they are supposed to have the things that they want, but a little hard work and sweat could never hurt a child, it gives them some kind of respect and understanding for the value of a dollar.

Anyway, one day my mother decided that we were going to move to Columbia, MO. I was a good five months along in my pregnancy but you couldn't tell. I busted out crying and exclaimed, "We can't move, we can't move!" My mother kept repeating, "Why not, why can't we move?" I was so scared, but I had to tell her. The words finally came out of my mouth… "Because

I'm pregnant." I was quiet as everyone looked at me with their mouths and eyes wide open. My mother said, "What? All this time and I'm thinking it's your sister out there having sex and it was you." My mother looked so disappointed in me. She looked over and said, "We are still moving." Next came the big question. "Who's the father, that big-headed boy you say you're going out with?" And of course, I said yes. I couldn't tell her the truth because he would never get out of prison if she found out. I know you're asking why couldn't she tell her mother the truth? Well, he was 23 years old when we were together. There I was, 15 years old and pregnant and moving away from everything I knew. Of course, people on the streets were talking. They were saying that my mom was moving me out of town because she was embarrassed by me being pregnant at such a young age. They had no clue that my mother didn't even know I was pregnant before she decided to move out of town.

There we were in a strange town and I was at a different school. By the way, they put me in a different school than all my siblings. It was an alternative school where all the bad kids, and of course, the pregnant ones, went. It was cool and they had a class to help us prepare for motherhood – I even had a midwife for delivery.

One day I had this sharp pain and it wasn't going away so I thought, oh Lord, am I in labor? We made it to the hospital but my contractions were too far apart, so they sent me home. I was at home in pain, trying to do homework as contractions kept coming. I was in intense pain so I went back to the hospital. The contractions still weren't close enough and I was not dilating. I went through that for three days and then they finally decided to keep me at the hospital. I was there for another 24 hours before the doctor decided to go in and break my water, and six hours later, a 6-pound, 8-ounce baby boy entered the world.

We named him De'vonte' Trevion Triblett. I said we because my mother took over that as soon as she found out I was having a boy. She said it was the boy that she never had. I looked up from my hospital bed and my family was looking at me like I did something wrong. I remember it like it was yesterday, my stepfather asked, "You sure that the baby daddy isn't white?" My son was so pale when he was born, he had yellow jaundice and he had to be placed in a glass case/bed under fluorescent lights. I also knew he was a lighter color because his father was also that color, but they didn't know that.

We ended up moving back to Sikeston a few months after my son was born. As soon as my old friend saw Tre, (that's my son's nickname) she said, "That's my uncle's baby." I looked at her and replied, "No it is not," and to my surprise, she told her uncle and he, of course, denied being the father. He felt that it couldn't be his baby because we were only together once. I am sure that's all it takes. As he went to prison two days after we were together, he just knew he wasn't the father. So of course, I had to get a DNA test and the test came back as 99.9% positive that he was the father. My son was then two years old and his father wouldn't be coming home for another two years.

Yes, I wanted to live my life as a teenager and hang out with my friends and I did, thanks to my family. Not only did they support me, but they pushed me as well. There is nothing like having the support of family. I didn't say that I was an angel…I gave my mother the blues. I was not hanging in the best of crowds, although I think people made us out to be much worse than what we were. I fought all the time, to the point that I was kicked out of high school. As I was a teen mom with no education and no back-up plan, I decided to do what everyone else was doing and that was hanging out, affiliating in gang activities, selling and doing drugs. That was not the life that I wanted to live, and I was determined not to become the statistic that the world had already figured that I was going to be, from having a child so young. I had dreams and I didn't want to become a product of my environment. My mom and stepfather did everything they could to provide for us, but it was hard to not be involved with what was around me every day. I learned that you don't have to be what the world or people perceive you to be; only you can stop you.

One day, it was like I had an epiphany or something and a light bulb came on. No, I wasn't a churchgoer at all, the Lord just had other plans for me. I had a serious talk with my mom and told her that I wanted to go to Job Corps, and I wanted to go to the one in Kansas City and not St. Louis, because it would be too close to home and I would be home every weekend and not stay focused. She asked me if I was sure if that was what I wanted and I said yes. She didn't question me any further and she arranged for me to go to Job Corps while she and the family watched my son. I left home focused and ready to take on what was ahead of me.

This was my first time away from home and my child, I had to tell myself every day that I needed this, and that Tre didn't ask to be here. He was a blessing from God and God gave him to me, so I had to do what I had to do. Honestly, I didn't know what I was doing, I just knew I had to do something different. Like I said earlier, I didn't know God for myself back then, and looking back on my life I know someone was praying for me.

I excelled while I was in Job Corps. I joined the Naval JROTC and that kept me busy and focused. One day, they had a bus that was taking students to the college to take the G.E.D. test and I decided to go, just in case something came up and I didn't manage to get to my diploma. The scores came back a few weeks later and I passed. I was so excited and surprised at the same time. I was also doing well in my trade which was Business Clerical. I had been at the campus for almost a year when I became the Vice-President of the campus; that's right, little ole me from Sikeston, Missouri...VP. I did so well by the time I received my diploma and certificate of training in October 1999, they were ready to hire me to work on the campus. I talked to my mom about it and she didn't like the idea at all because she couldn't see me and my son six hours away from her. I did not want to move back to Sikeston, so we agreed that we would move back to Columbia and start over.

Not only did I want to start over, but I had also decided that I was going to join the military. I was working with a female Navy Recruiter, doing odd things for her including babysitting and helping her run errands. I finally went in and took the test and passed, and the only thing that I had to do then was to find a job and swear in. Before doing that though, I had a long conversation with my stepfather because he served in the Army. I learned from early on that it doesn't hurt to ask questions or to turn to the elders in your family or your life, for advice. He explained to me that if I joined the Navy that I could be gone for up to six months at times, without seeing my son. He let me know that if I joined the Army, Tre could at least come with me. My Naval Recruiter was not happy with me at all, as I had completed everything with her, and then decided to go to a different branch of service. I swore in on July 31, 2000, with a report date of September 6, 2000.

While all of this was going on, my son's father was released from prison. Tre was now four years old and his father approached me and asked to be in our lives. I let him know that I didn't trust him or believe that he was ready to be in a committed relationship. After about three months of him pursuing me, I gave in. He asked me to marry him and I said yes! My mother did not agree with this at all. She said, "I told you to give him a chance, not to marry him." She was right. I didn't know him for real, but I was grown, and you couldn't tell me anything.

It was time for me to report to Basic Training in Fort Leonard Wood, MO, where I would complete both Basic Training and Advanced Individual Training. I would be there for a total of four months. The training was intense and all I wanted was support from my so-called fiancé. However, every time I called him he was too busy to talk. As a matter of fact, he probably only wrote me three times out of the entire four months. After completing my training, I called everything off with him. But even though I called it off, I still slept with him again before going to my first duty station in Fort Polk, Louisiana.

It had been about three months since I reported to Fort Polk and we were out in the field and I vomited all over the place. I knew I was pregnant. What you don't know is that I had only been intimate with my child's father a total of three times in my life and I conceived two kids by him. How is that even possible? Now, what was I going to do? I had just got there and I was pregnant again. I had called off the engagement and was in another state away from my family and friends. I was in over my head and considered getting out of the military due to hardship, but a Platoon Sergeant stepped in and treated me like his daughter and asked me the right questions. He said, "What you going to do, get out, go back home to your momma? You already have one child and pregnant with another and you think the best thing for you to do is give up? You did all this for a reason…you came here to do something different for your life. Don't give up; stay in, if not for yourself, for your kids." We need people like that to come in and show us the big picture. Sometimes, we get caught up in what we are going through and cannot see anything ahead of us. He changed my life forever. You know who you are. I love and appreciate you from the bottom of my heart.

After going through all of that, I decided to stay in the military and take my ex back. Once things were arranged for him to come to Louisiana, he came. I forgot to mention that another reason why I called off the engagement was due to him having a relationship with someone else while I was in training and she was supposed to be pregnant. Of course, he denied it.

I had my daughter, Kiona Ashunti Lott, on October 4, 2001. Her delivery was not as bad as Tre's, she popped right on out. We changed Tre's last name from Triblett to Lott after Kiona was born. We were so excited about and blessed by our healthy new baby.

We got married about a month or so after Kiona was born. There were plenty of signs telling me not to go through with it, and even the judge asked me if I was sure. He knew my fiancé from his previous appearances in front of him. I decided to go through with it anyway. My goodness, the things I know now that I wish I knew back then! I went back to him because I thought that was the right thing to do. I had two kids by him, but I really didn't know him and doing it for the kids was the wrong reason. Family members reminded me that another woman was supposedly having his baby.

One day, I walked out to the mailbox and guess what had arrived…a paternity test. When did he take a paternity test? This is what I asked myself as I opened the letter and it said that he was 99.9% the father. I lost my cool and kicked him out, sending him back to his mother. He had always been a momma's boy who could never do anything wrong, even though he had been in and out of prison all his life. There I was at 21 years old with two kids, far from home.

A couple of months went by and I received the order to report to Germany. My husband had been calling and writing to ask to get back together during this time. I looked at it like this – why not try to work it out and get back together? We would be going to a different country where no one knew us, and it would give us a chance to start over. You can have it in your head that things are going to be better, and then reality kicks in.

We arrived in Frankfurt, Germany, on January 27, 2003, and I had never seen so much snow in my life. We made it to our destination of, Hanau, Germany, I reported in, and within two weeks I received orders to go to the war in Iraq. We were in another country with no family or friends and we hadn't even received our household goods or car yet.

One day, when I was getting off work, my husband called me to let me know that Kiona was sick and we needed to take her to the hospital. I wasn't in my vehicle and was catching a ride with someone. In wintertime in Germany, the snow is crazy. He was calling me repeatedly to get home so we could take our daughter to the hospital. The last time he called, he said that I needed to hurry up, and I was trying to get home. I guess he didn't like what was going on in the background because he expressed that while I was out having fun, we had a sick child at the house. When I made it to the house, he charged towards me like a raging bull and the only thing I could do was hit him. We interlocked with one another. I looked at him, he looked at me, and he knew that was it. I was not going to be in a relationship where I was out working all day and had to come home to foolishness. I went to my superiors the next day and let them know what happened and that I wanted to send him back to the United States. It sounded good but they were not hearing me. I had orders to report to Iraq and that is where I was going. Long story short, he got to stay while I was gone to the war. I was over there for a total of nine months. I had an opportunity to get promoted while I was there and I wrote and called my husband, begging and pleading with him to send me the documents that were needed to get my promotion. He never sent them. I thought long and hard about everything and concluded that if he was not with me, he was against me.

I had this one Staff Sergeant that always tried to get me to go to church, although I was so caught up with hanging out at a club/tent called the Dusty Room. This Sergeant was persistent, and he was on me, and I am glad he was. I went to his church one Sunday and it was like something I had never seen before. One guy fell and no one went to attend to him, they just let him lay there. I was spooked, to be honest. They said that he was filled with the Holy Ghost and they were allowing the Lord to do his work within him. I didn't fully understand, but I was interested. I started attending church services more than the club and I allowed myself to get to know me. I started reading my bible more and listened to more worship and gospel music. About four months after I started going to church, we got the news that we were going home. I was so excited about seeing my babies! Kiona was only two years old when I left her. When we landed, all of the families were there including mine, and we even appeared in the newspaper; a picture of me, my husband, and my baby.

I wasn't home for more than four days when I told my husband that I wanted a divorce. I had had more than enough time to weigh my Pros and Cons while I was in Iraq, and I decided that I wanted more, and I didn't have to settle for what I had decided for myself or my children. I thought about what harm being in a single mother household and not having their father around would do to them, and I decided that I was not going to stay for the kids. I was not going to stay in a marriage that wasn't built on love.

Before I decided this, I had an opportunity to go to the church he was attending. Unlike myself, my ex-husband grew up in the church. When we were in Fort Polk, he used to always use the Word to get the things that he wanted or try to make me feel like I wasn't doing my womanly duties. I didn't understand the Bible but that made me start reading it to gain my own understanding. I tried to attend church while I was stationed in Fort Polk, but it was strange and they did strange things while I was attending like all the women had to sit on one side and the men on the other, even married couples. I didn't know the Word, but what I did know was God wouldn't bring a couple together and separate them in His house. So, my journey with the Lord started way before that Sergeant approached me. I just wasn't ready. I attended the ministry he was attending even after I sent him back to the United States as I was so interested in getting to know more about God and his Son, Jesus.

Shortly after making it back, we received orders to escort the President, in Normandy. When we got there, I didn't get detailed for work so I had an opportunity to tour Paris. I went to the beach and there was a group of people there, in Bible study. I had never paid attention to this before, but now everywhere I went, someone was talking about Jesus. That's when I decided that I wanted to do it. I was no longer in control of my life and I whole-heartedly wanted to give my life to Christ.

When we made it back home, I was pumping myself up to go to the altar. I got to the church and I was ready, but when I arrived, they announced that we were going to have a guest speaker from Africa. In my mind, I thought no, no, no, this is going to mess up everything, this is supposed to be my moment. I had planned how I thought things should go, but what I didn't know was I was about to see and experience God's power in a way that I could never imagine.

The pastor started preaching and I had never heard the Word spoken like this before. I felt a tugging to go to the altar and I did. I remember the First Lady coming down to the floor where I was and I whispered that what was about to happen to me, not everyone needed to see. They took me to the pastor's chambers where I remember all the Elders, Deacons, Deaconesses, and I'm sure more leaders, surrounded me, and they were praying and having me repent for things as they came to my mind. I was coughing up phlegm and foaming from the mouth and it felt like someone was choking me when I tried to speak. I also remember my heart felt like it was trying to jump out of my chest as it was turning flips in there. One of the leaders grabbed me and she held me and prayed, and although I don't remember it all, what I do know is that she told me that I hadn't let go completely and God had more work to do. I thought I was in that room for like 15 minutes. Turns out, I was in there for four hours.

I woke up the next morning and I couldn't stop saying, "Thank you, Jesus, thank you, Jesus, thank you, Jesus." I needed something from the store and I decided to walk. I never walked because I didn't need to, I had a car, but something that day told me to take a walk. As I began to walk up the street, something told me to go back to the house into my kitchen and look in the top cabinet on the left. I went home and did just that. There was a shoebox in the cabinet and I grabbed the box, which was full of Muslim paraphernalia, including the Koran and tapes, which had to belong to my ex-husband. I'm not saying that there is anything wrong with that religion, it's just not what I believe in. I took that box outside to the dumpster and the following Sunday, I was fully delivered.

I can honestly say that my life has not been the same since I finally decided to give my heart to the Lord. I'm telling you this to say be careful of who you affiliate yourself with, who you give your heart to, and who you accept into your space. You must understand that whatever burden they carry, you will carry that burden as well. I never knew my ex-husband read the Koran, let alone had one in our home, and me not knowing what I was holding on to, was keeping me from my deliverance.

ABOUT THE AUTHOR

Renata Triblett is a US Army (SFC) Retiree, CEO of H3r Clozet Boutique, and a Certified Life Coach. She attends Strayer University and is studying for her bachelor's degree in Business Management with a concentration in Management/Entrepreneurship. She resides in Georgia with her young daughter Kiona Lott, and her son De'vonte' Lott lives in Texas.

CHAPTER 13

Gracefully Broken

by Zen Watson

"Gracefully Broken is to be broken by God so that He can take you to a new level with him, to be broken so that God can promote you and put you in a place where you can experience a new blessing, to be used and filled by Him. ... When God uses grace to break you, it means He is about to add favor in your life."

Have you ever been faced with challenges in life and wondered, "How did I stay so strong?" Well, that is what I've been wondering for the past eight years.

I know that right now things probably aren't going as planned, but I want to let you know that your circumstances will and can change. Keep the faith, keep the faith! I can share my testimony because of the man above and because I learned the importance of having "faith as small as a mustard seed."

For many years I asked, "WHY ME?" Hey, why not me? After a 10-year relationship with the kid's father, experiencing domestic violence, and battling depression from my past, I was ready for this dark cloud that was hovering over me to be gone. From the time I was a little girl, I pictured myself married, living in a big house with a Jeep, car, and motorcycle in my driveway, not to mention a good-paying job with savings. However, there I was, 27 years of age, emotionally and spiritually broken, no money, no house, no car, nothing, and to top it off, I am a single mother.

I thought this man was my knight in shining armor. I gave him 10 years. I loved him and saw myself with him forever until he threatened the kid's lives. This is when my story took a different path compared to the one I wished for at 12 years old. Before I go into more detail, let me start with when we first met.

Phillip was the new guy at my job. When I saw him walk past the cafeteria door, I thought to myself, "Who is that?" Tall, handsome, with fresh braids, looking like a younger Snoop Dogg with gold teeth. He wasn't there when I left on a vacation to New York just weeks prior. I kept asking his friend Gerrard to hook me up, but he acted as if I wasn't serious.

One day, my workmates and I were in the break room talking and laughing, nothing but vibez. In walked my crush. Oh, my goodness, butterflies swarmed in my tummy. He explained that his shift was over and said his goodbyes. My workmates dared me to make the first move. "You gotta be kidding me!" Right?

Women don't make the first move, the man is supposed to do the chasing and besides, I was the type to play hard to get. I acted all confident, "Oh, you think I can't ask for his number? Ok, watch me!" I quietly walked into the female's changing room, which was next to the men's. What was I about to do? I was a shy person when it came to men and dating. I heard the door to the men's changing room open. "It's now or never," I thought, as I popped my head around the corner. "Hey!" I called. He looked back at me. "You got a girl?" I asked. "No," he replied, "Can I have your number?" "Yup." I grabbed my bag and emptied it onto the floor in search of a pen. Smiling, I used my left hand as paper to write down his number. Laughing, I went back into the break room to show my coworkers that I had gotten his number. Hahaha!

Later that night, I took a shower and washed the number off my hand. When I saw him again days later, I wrote his number on paper and then, I lost that too! What was going on? Zen was prepared the third time around! I had my phone with me that day so I immediately entered his number into my contacts.

Little did I know, it was a sign from the jump, Phillip wasn't the one. During our relationship, my mother once said, "That boy is going to kill you one day!" It almost came to pass. NO JOKE!

He gave me great babies though, so I'm grateful for that.

As we got to know each other over the next few weeks, I found out he was in a little situationship. His ex was pregnant, but he didn't know if it was his. One of my coworkers told me not to entertain him due to that situation, but he was open and honest about it so hey, why not? Two months later, we made it official.

During the honeymoon period, I was honestly happy. We had picnics in the park, rented movies from Blockbusters, and enjoyed all kinds of snacks for movie night. We had a few things in common, so we were happy. Unknown to him, I was battling my own demons.

From the time she was a little girl, my mother suffered from depression to the point that when life got too challenging for her, Mother would say she felt like killing herself. She was going to jump over the balcony. As a child, it was scary because you didn't know if she was serious or not.

The story is about to get juicy! Are you ready?

"Beyond the Smile" was a lot of sadness and confusion. Mom was always sad about something; she found fault in everything I did or said. Unnecessary arguments led to me getting kicked out a lot. I am not an argumentative person, so arguing all the time kills my spirit and weakens my energy. The day I tried to kill myself, I was emotionally drained. It was a Sunday. My mother called my job and told my boss some of my personal business which was so embarrassing, to say the least. If it wasn't one thing it was another. She accused me of having sex. Maybe I was, but not that night, and I was above the legal age so if I was, so what?

On my arrival home that night after work, this miserable woman was going off. "Why can't she leave me alone?" I thought. "Always picking at me…like damn!" Then she had the nerve to say, "You want to hit me?" She only dared to say that to me because she knew I wouldn't, but my older sister, who had Mom's energy, she would be ready to whoop-ass. Whenever Mom had an outburst, she would spew hurtful things and then try to justify it by saying, "It's because I love you." That is toxic love if you ask me, so it's no wonder I gravitated to the same toxic love in my relationships. Hell, I obviously didn't know any better. When Phillip and I would fight, he would say the same things, "I LOVE YOU. I WON'T DO IT AGAIN." Lies, upon lies! I should have left after the first hit.

We need to be careful about what we say and do while we are angry. You never know how it will make the other person feel at that moment. Mom said things like she regretted having daughters and there was nothing she was proud of when it came to us, and she would call me illiterate and tell me that I would amount to nothing. Unknown to my mother, those vile words that came out of her mouth made my brain explode like a pressure cooker. While sitting on my bed with my head in my hands, I would think, "How can I make her stop or leave me alone?"

Then suddenly, she told me to, "Get out!" GET OUT…Where was I to go? I was 17. I had been living with my mother since I was eight years old. It was 1992 when I moved to the United Kingdom.

Growing up, I always wished she had left me in Jamaica. I was happier there. I went from living in a nice house with my aunt, her husband, Marshall, and their three children to living in a room with Mom and my older sister. And we moved twice after that.

My life growing up in the UK was challenging and my relationship with my mother was horrific.

After many long years of fighting battles within myself, at the age of 34, I asked God to heal me. I was ready to break this generational curse. Now that I have given you an insight into the back story which leads up to my suicide attempt, let me get back to the story of the mother acting out.

After a long day at work, what you want is to come home to some peace. But my mother came into my room screaming for me to leave while throwing my stuff all over the room. She grabbed my phone and charger and pulled it so hard it broke, cursed some more, and then left the room. Shattered and alone in my room, I saw only darkness.

Mom had a friend who was staying with us by the name of Sharon. Both her and Mom were about to leave for church one morning when Sharon came to inform me not to leave but to stay until she got back. Little did they know that that would have been the last time they saw me had things gone my way. I had planned to end my life the minute they drove off. I had nothing to live for. I was going to give my mother what she wished for; she didn't want a daughter and I had enough of her, so hey… it was a win-win situation. I let out a sigh of relief as I heard them leave. I could breathe a little better now. I watched as Mom's car drove away as she headed for church. It was time. I went into the kitchen and got all the pills I could find in the drawers. As much as I loved the Lord, it was time for the grim reaper to hold my hand. Young Zen walked back up to her room crying, and then, she took every one of those pills.

Boom! The next morning my eyes opened. WHAT? I'm still here? OMG, I was ready to leave. Imagine my heartbreak, imagine this mess and not to mention, I had to go to work that day! How was I going to walk for 30 minutes from my house to catch the train and travel over an hour, and then walk another

10 minutes to my job? It crossed my mind that I should call and opt out of work as I was running back and forth from the bathroom, spitting up green liquid. The taste was bitter and totally yuk. I could hardly move. Why was I still alive? I was MAD! I should have been worried about my mother's reaction but I didn't care when or if she found out what I had done. I continued to run from my room to the bathroom, trying to get dressed for work, but in the end, I decided to let Sharon know about what I did. Well, of course, Sharon called my mother. Within a few minutes, the ambulance pulled up. They were about to leave with me inside when suddenly a car pulled up and all I heard was, "You're wicked, you're wicked! You know I suffer from depression." I went deaf after that. WAH! WAH! WAH! How selfish of her to be thinking about herself at this point. What about me? To me, this was confirmation. Mom really didn't want me and to be completely honest here, she still feels that way some 18 years later.

Why me? Man, what did I do that was so bad that I deserved this? I had been a happy little girl from Jamaica, a nice hot place, where after church and dinner, I would get ice cream from the ice cream man, who rode on a motorcycle with a box on the back that contained many different flavors. I still remember as a kid running towards it to get him to stop. I remember playing on the grass in front of my aunt and uncle's restaurant and bar. I would sit and stare at the blue skies while the airplanes flew by and my cousins and I would wave as if the people in the air could see us. From that to a cold, miserable-looking country, where my life had turned upside down.

Looking back on it now, it was all part of the process. My story makes my testimony even greater and my triumphs even more amazing. I achieved something I never thought I would, and I give all the glory to the man above because he was with me during all the ups and downs.

The connection between my son's father and I did not last. Although he was there during the challenges of my early years, we didn't have the best relationship. Ten years, three engagement rings, and two children later, I ended it after he threatened twice to stab the boys. I knew I had to get my kids and myself out of that toxic relationship. I was fortunate because my sisters on my father's side helped relocate me to the USA shortly after.

In the first three years, I was stagnant, with no car, no house of my own, and I lived with one of my sisters and her family. Before my move, I had only met this sister twice in my whole life. Although I didn't know her well, you couldn't tell by the way we acted and treated each other.

I went from babysitting for $30 a week to cleaning a school for $160 a week. I tried to get work at Motel 6, but they were unable to pay me under the table and I didn't have the necessary papers yet to be legally hired. However, with the help of family and friends I have made it through the tough years.

In my third year in the USA, I decided to fast for the things the boys and I lacked. I fasted in January and that April I began to reap the harvest. God blessed me with a car, so I no longer had to ask my sister or friends to borrow theirs. Then I got a house. God was so good to us. He blessed us with an amazing couple who never asked about my legal status, nor did they ask for a deposit to move in just the first month's rent. The way this blessing came about was when I was cleaning the home and office of their daughter-in-law, she told me her in-laws had a rental property and were seeking tenants. I was grinding hard that summer to make ends meet, but I won't complain about it too much because if I had to, I would do it all over again. I kept my promise to my kids to get a place of our own and I did it.

Due to the stresses of life, our utilities got cut off and we lived in darkness for a while – three months to be exact. Still, I made the best of it. Candles and cold showers, and I would tell the boys, "We are all we got, so mommy will make it work, no complaints." Yes, I could have run to my sister for help, but I didn't. I kept the faith through it all.

Through the help and guidance from another amazing lady at the church I attend, Tabernacle of Praise, I became a Certified Life Coach. This happened after a lady who I affectionately call Queen Mother, had organized a women's retreat that I was able to attend. It was an amazing experience, and it was there I found my moments to release years of baggage, and to break the generational stronghold that had plagued me for so long. I was now confident to let my mother know, if she couldn't respect me as a person, I would have to distance myself from her and I was not playing. Every time I spoke to her, I felt sad afterward. Many have encouraged me to speak with her, but I honestly don't see any reason to. Our relationship is just too toxic for me. I need peace and good energy in my circle. I need people around me that will uplift my spirit instead of breaking it.

Two years before I met my current husband, I returned to Atlanta and found myself in another bad relationship; another case of choosing the wrong guy. This time, I ended up homeless, sitting at McDonald's with my sons asking myself again, "How did I end up here?" Throughout the whole ordeal, I kept telling the boys, "Stay positive, think positive, we are good. God got us, and we are going to be alright, don't you worry about nothing!"

I reached out to Queen Mother, aka Minister Chris Scott, and asked if she would pray for us. She asked if I was ok. "Of course," I replied hastily. She then invited me to have the boys take part in summer camp. She felt it would help them keep their minds off the current situation at home. Home? We had no home. I was staying in a roach motel. In any event, I agreed to drop the boys off on the first day of camp, with the summer camp leader, Samantha.

I needed advice so I contacted Minister Chris again. She asked if I could go to see another amazing lady, Pastor Tongela Smith. I wasn't sure that I could as I had no transportation.

Then I thought about the babysitter's folks. I called them and he and his wife willingly came and picked me up. They gave me hope at that moment, the kind of hope and extra faith that I needed. It was a 45-minute drive to the Salvation Army where Pastor Smith worked. She called around, found a shelter for us, and connected me with another great soul, Pastor Lett.

The babysitter's father and mother waited with me until everything was in order at the Salvation Army. Nothing but blessings on blessings!

We had our own beds! Access to hot showers, meals, laundry rooms, etc. Although we had an eight o'clock curfew, I had no complaints. I was grateful. Every day, I would encourage the boys to live a life of gratitude with no complaints. My sister Shahara is the prayer warrior for the family and has been my rock over the years. She had expressed her concerns about us being in the shelter but I would tell her, "Don't you worry 'bout us, things are going to change for me and the boys, you just keep praying for us." One of the rules of the shelter was to find a job and seek alternative accommodations as they only provide 31 days of emergency stay. Giyahni, the youngest, expressed his concerns about us having 21 days left at the shelter. I informed him that we weren't going to worry about the days we had left, we would embrace every day with positive thoughts and good energy.

One day, I happened to be walking past the American Deli and the door had a hiring sign on it. I walked past thinking, "They wouldn't hire me." Looking at the kids, I asked them if they thought I should apply. "Yes, Mom!" So, I went in, filled out the application and we left. A couple of hours later, the head cashier Toni called to say she would give me a try. Toni explained, "You only have two days to catch on to the register." Well, I achieved that goal and within a few weeks, I received several pay raises. Over the next few weeks, I made it to work by taking a local taxi.

One day while talking with my roommate, I said to Justine, "You never know, I might meet my husband in the American Deli. So, said! So, done! #Speak Life! During my time working there, an older gentleman sent his goddaughter in to give me his number. I paid him no mind, my focus was getting the kids in school and finding a place to live and I didn't need or want any distractions. However, he was persistent and would hold small talk whenever he came in. One day this man that had been trying to get my attention came in talking loudly on his phone. I asked his goddaughter what he did for a living and she said construction. As I did have some construction experience, I thought I'd ask about a job. I could use more income. When he got off the phone, I asked if he was hiring. The gentleman quickly said, "YES." OH, snap! Now I had to ask for the number again. He gave it and I texted him my information straight away. He quickly replied that I could come over to his house for an interview after I had finished work.

To be honest, I wasn't feeling that, and I made up several excuses. "My taxi couldn't come." He said, "I will come get you." "Oh, but I have my kids." "I have a theater room where they can watch movies or TV." I sat down on a bench contemplating what to do. A few minutes later, the guy pulls up. On my end, I was there for the job, but I quickly discovered he had me there to interview to be his wife, the wife he had been asking God to bless him with for years. I was upfront with him. Due to a car crash months before, I had lost my vehicle and I needed the extra income to get another one and a place to live. Then he showed me his two vacant rooms and offered them to me. Once again, I wasn't so sure, especially because of the kids. "Who is this man and where did he come from?" I wondered.

A few days later, I received notice it was now time to leave the shelter. My 31 days were up but Pastor Lett gave me an extra 18 days. I called Arthur, the man I had met in the American Deli, and he wasn't surprised because I had told him the day of the interview that my days to stay at the shelter were coming to an end. After work, he came and picked up my youngest and me from the shelter. Then he drove to Enterprise and reserved a car for me to pick up on a Thursday. Again, "Who is this man and where did he come from?" Thursday arrived and Arthur picked me up about 8:30 a.m. after the boys left for school and we drove to Enterprise. The salesclerk had reserved a white jeep for me. Wow, God is good!

I told Arthur I would not move in straight away because I wanted to give the boys and me more time to get to know him. While I was at work, he would get the boys from the shelter after the school bus dropped them off and bring them to me at work. By this time, I was working double shifts and was now the lead cashier, so I had no other choice but to have them with me during my shifts. On the days I finished at 4:00 p.m., I asked if I could come over to cook a meal, as we were not able to cook at the shelter. He loved that; a woman that can cook, most men loved that idea.

I started going back to the shelter but the boys by this time did not want to leave. Weeks later, when I asked the boys about our next move, without hesitation they said they wanted to move in with Mr. Arthur. I was still being cautious about this man. I spoke with him about renting one of his spare rooms to a lady I had met at the shelter and who was about to become homeless like myself. I guess it was my way of feeling more secure living with him. I had also hired her to work with me at the deli and I made sure she was straight. We moved in. Arthur then stopped renting the car and bought me…a Jeep Grand Cherokee. Four months later, we were married. I finally met Mr. Right! A man that when he said, "I got you," he meant it.

My journey has been far from easy but through it all, I kept the faith! The man above watched over us every day and he still does. I give him all the praise because that invisible energy gave me the strength I needed when I didn't have it. Even on those days that I was close to giving up, he kept me. I hope that my testimony gives you the strength and motivation to keep going. Keep pushing and keep moving in the direction that the man above has planned for you. What worked for me during my trials was gratitude. I am grateful for all the people in my life, good and bad. If it were not for the bumps in the road, I wouldn't be as appreciative as I am today.

It has been a year since I met my husband, and I am so grateful for him not giving up on me. He takes care of me and the kids the best he can and because of him, our lives have changed for the better. I was a single mother who came from a broken place; an illegal immigrant who didn't take no for an answer; a strong Black woman that "Beyond the Smile" kept fighting to live and to be her best self, even with all her wounds and scars.

Follow your dreams and don't let anything stop you from achieving them. No one said life would be easy. Keep pushing yourself and keep the faith even when it's hard to. I have a lot of people to thank. If it weren't for my family and friends, the ones that stuck by me through it all without wavering, I wouldn't be where I am today. I am forever grateful. You never know how strong you are until being strong is your only option.

I love you,
Zen

ABOUT THE AUTHOR

Zen Watson is a respected entrepreneur, community change agent, and a Certified Life Coach.

Her passion for people developed at the age of 21 while working at a youth center called, Coin Street, in the United Kingdom. It was through that experience that her heart became open to the needs of others.

Zen, who identifies herself as an overcomer, is not afraid to help people tackle the most daunting and challenging parts of their story. She uses her personal experiences with depression, domestic violence, molestation, and being a single mother to empower and encourage others toward wholeness.

She is gifted with an innate ability to listen and truly hear the hearts of men, women, children, and teens to help them live their very best lives. Her goal is to motivate and inspire others while leaving a legacy of kindness, love, peace, and laughter.

Made in the USA
Coppell, TX
22 March 2021